Blue's Clues

FOR SUCCESS

Blue's Clues

FOR SUCCESS

THE 8 SECRETS BEHIND A PHENOMENAL BUSINESS

Diane Tracy

Dearborn™
Trade Publishing
A **Kaplan Professional** Company

Vice President and Publisher: Cynthia A. Zigmund
Editorial Director: Donald J. Hull
Senior Acquisitions Editor: Jean Iversen
Senior Managing Editor: Jack Kiburz
Interior Design: Lucy Jenkins
Cover Design: Jody Billert, Billert Communications
Typesetting: the dotted i

Published by Dearborn Trade Publishing, a Kaplan Professional Company

Printed in the United States of America

02   03   04   10   9   8   7   6   5   4   3   2   1

Library of Congress Cataloging-in-Publication Data
Tracy, Diane.
    Blue's clues for success : the 8 secrets behind a phenomenal business
  / Diane Tracy.
        p.   cm.
    Includes index.
    ISBN 0-7931-5376-X (hardcover)
    1. Success in business—Handbooks, manuals, etc.   I. Title.
    HF5386 .T8143 2002
    650.1—dc21   2002001824

To Angela, Traci, Alice, Jen, Dave, Wendy, and the entire *Blue's Clues* staff. You are the finest team I have ever met.

ACKNOWLEDGMENTS

The writing of this book was an exercise in collaboration, which is one of the hallmarks of the *Blue's Clues* and Nickelodeon culture. I thank Herb Scannell and the Nickelodeon senior staff for granting me access to the information I needed to write an accurate account of the *Blue's Clues* story.

Many people at Nickelodeon were generous with their time and support in giving me interviews, verifying facts, helping me secure visuals, and in a number of other ways. They include: Leigh Ann Brodsky, Janice Burgess, Bob Charde, Anita Chinkes, Maude Divittis, Amy Drake, Karen Driscoll, Samantha Freeman, Leslie Freeman, Jessica Grabarz, Freddie Greenberg, Albee Hecht, Russell Hicks, Brown Johnson, Dan Martinsen, Margaret Milnes, Theresa O'Neal, Veronica Proctor, Kyra Reppen, Stuart Rosenstein, David Schliecker, Jessica Schwartz, Andra Shapiro, Lauren Sklar, Marsha Williams, and Steve Youngwood. I'm sure there were others, so I apologize to those I may have omitted.

I also thank Jonathan Hochwald, Liz McDonald, Shoshana Kovac, Michael Rubin, Nick Balaban, Dan Anderson, Jennings Bryant, Amy Jordan, Peggy Charren, Nelson Torres, Stacey Levin, Ruth Sarlin, Catherine Mullally, Tom Mizer, Shannon McQuillan, and Kelly Leahy for their cooperation and support. A special thanks goes to Tom Johnson.

Many thanks to my editor, Jean Iversen, and the Dearborn staff for their belief in this project from the very beginning. To Mark LeBlanc for his wise advice and steadying influence when the way seemed unclear.

This book was written in a very short time period, which required a lot of cooperation from the *Blue's Clues* staff. Thanks to

Angela Santomero, Traci Paige Johnson, Alice Wilder, Jennifer Twomey, Dave Palmer, and Wendy Harris for sticking with me through the entire project, for giving so generously of their time, and for being the wonderful people that they are. Without them, this book would not have been written.

Former host Steve Burns and current host Donovan Patton were also helpful in the writing of this book. Thanks to Amy Horton, Julie Epstein, Amy Steinberg, Amy Gutell, and Catherine Alcoran for their administrative support. A special thanks to Soo Kim for her help with the graphics and visuals and to staff members who helped me understand what it's like to work at *Blue's Clues*—David Bouffard, Ian Chernichaw, Dale Clowdis, Scott Dodson, Alex Fogarty, Shannon George, Sarah Landy, Michael Lapinski, Amanda Latrell, Karen Leavitt, Andrew Levin, David Levy, Jessica Lissy, Khalida Katz Lockheed, Adam Peltzman, Marcy Pritchard, Astrid Riemer, Tatia Rosenthal, Alison Sherman, Amy Steinberg, and John Terhorst.

The person I owe the biggest thanks to is my husband, Peter Sage, who lost a wife during the writing of this book. Thanks for keeping me going during the long days and nights. You are the best.

Blue's Clues is Nickelodeon's breakthrough television show for preschoolers that has changed the way they watch television. Since its first episode in 1996, *Blue's Clues* has become a phenomenon that reaches 13.7 million viewers each week. It is one of the most-watched shows among preschoolers, bigger than *Sesame Street, Barney and Friends,* and *Arthur.* It has spawned international versions in the United Kingdom and Korea and airs in 60 countries. The show has even become a campy hit in some college dorms.

Educators love it; parents love it. Celebrity fans Rosie O'Donnell, Gloria Estefan, Marlee Matlin, and Julia Louis-Dreyfus have made cameo appearances. It has become so much a part of pop culture that it is the subject of *Saturday Night Live* jokes and comic strips. It has received numerous awards, including nine Emmy nominations. The show has spawned a host of other businesses, including a live theatrical show, books, videos, CDs, and a vast array of consumer products. The brand is so strong, it has sold more than $3 billion in consumer products since 1998.

WHO THIS BOOK IS FOR

Maybe you've heard of *Blue's Clues,* maybe you haven't. It doesn't matter. This is a story for everyone. If you are a business leader, manager, or team leader, this book will show you how to:

- Develop a strong vision, translate it into every part of your business, and use it to inspire your people to greatness.

Actress Marlee Matlin shows former host, Steve, and Blue some basic sign language during a cameo appearance on the show.

- Move your product or service from "successful" to "phenomenal" by creating a strong brand.

- Delight and please your customers in ways you never imagined.

- Develop real teams that create powerful synergies and result in greater innovation, increased efficiencies, and skyrocketing productivity.

- Create a culture that attracts and keeps the best talent.

Best of all, this book will provide you with a holistic approach to creating business and personal success. Using the 8 Secrets to Business Success model, I will show you how to create amazing synergies by integrating all the disciplines in the eight-clue model.

If you are a person who is searching for a sense of meaning and fulfillment in your life and career; if you know you have some greatness within you that is dying to find expression; or, better put, if you feel a piece of your soul will die if you don't find it—then this book is for you. It's a story that will make you get up and out of your seat; it will change the way you think about the obstacles facing you in your life; and it will inspire you to believe that anything is possible, which, by the way, is exactly what the television show does for children.

If you are a parent or educator, you will learn what child development experts and researchers say about the show, and why it has captivated the hearts and minds of children everywhere. You'll understand the multitude of sophisticated ways the show fosters thinking skills, problem-solving skills, and emotional and social development.

WHY I WROTE THIS BOOK

As a consultant, speaker, and coach to executives in Fortune 500 companies and beyond for more than 18 years, I have worked with thousands of executives and companies all over the world. While I have many wonderful clients who are doing a lot of things right—organizations such as the Office of Central Operations for the Social Security Administration, for one—most of the management/business books I have written were inspired by all the things I see that leaders and companies are *not* doing.

It's interesting. Walk into any major bookstore and you will see that there is no shortage of books on business and management. Leaders of organizations have access to more information about how to create and sustain a successful business than ever before. But what they know intellectually, what they believe in their hearts, and what they are able to execute, are all too often light years apart.

Nickelodeon's *Blue's Clues* is one of the few companies in all my years of experience that actually lives the principles I wrote about in my previous management books—*Truth, Trust, and the Bottom Line, The Ten Steps to Empowerment,* and *The First Book of Common Sense Management.* The leaders truly walk the talk, live the vision, and are expert in every single aspect of their business.

As you read the *Blue's Clues* story, you will probably think, "This is too good to be true." I thought the same thing when I first started working with *Blue's Clues* as a consultant—no one could be this smart, this disciplined, and so pure in motive, all at the same time. I looked for some glaring weakness and could not find it. It wasn't something I was accustomed to seeing in corporate America.

Nickelodeon did not pay me to write this book. I am writing it because I truly love this group of young people and am inspired by what they have achieved. They have a powerful message to share with leaders and companies everywhere, both in terms of how to create a phenomenal financial success and how to create a work environment where people love to come to work and feel good about themselves and what they do.

HOW THIS BOOK IS DIFFERENT

If this book looks a little offbeat, unlike a typical business book, it is so by design. I realize I am taking a risk—some may pass it up because it doesn't look serious enough—but I don't want this book to look like every other business book on the shelf. I think business-book readers are looking for something refreshingly different. Don't let the elementary nature of the show mislead you—there is a very sophisticated, powerful business message behind the show's success.

I know you don't have a lot of time to read books like this. That's why I have tried to be laser-beam efficient in the delivery of the message by keeping the format simple and words to a minimum. Like the show itself, this book is designed so that you can go back to it again and again and get something out of it.

HOW TO USE THIS BOOK

Throughout this book I will be telling the *Blue's Clues* story—what they did and how they did it. And then I will translate their story into principles and guidelines you can apply to achieve phenomenal success in your own company, team, career, or life.

The book content is organized around the 8 Secrets to Business Success model, the eight-step model that shows all the disciplines employed in *Blue's Clues* and ways they came together synergistically to create magic and business success. Each chapter provides one of the clues to the show's success. At the end of each chapter are suggestions for how you can apply the principles outlined in the chapter to your own business as well as to your personal life.

"The Personal Story" sidebars throughout the book will introduce you to some of the people behind the show. By telling their personal stories, the hope is you'll find inspiration for your own life and career. You'll even hear from "Steve," the original live-action host who left the show, and his replacement, "Joe" who stepped onto the scene in April 2002.

Maybe you know a *Blue's Clues* customer; maybe you don't. If you don't, I thought you might like to hear from some audience members. Their stories, as relayed by their parents, appear in "The Audience Speaks" sidebars. Some of their stories are hilarious and some are profoundly moving, but all of them point to the big impact this little show has had on children everywhere.

THE BOTTOM LINE

As you read this story, you may wonder where the young creators of the show got their inspiration to do what they did. It's simple. They got it from their customers—two- to five-year-olds.

One of the by-products of growing into adulthood is that we lose the heart of a child and we complicate matters. So many of our natural instincts such as joy, openness, curiosity, imagination, and playfulness—the very qualities that are intrinsic to an innovative, successful business and fulfilling life—are sadly programmed right out of us.

All you have to do is walk the halls of the *Blue's Clues* offices and studio and you know you are among a rare group of people who have found a way to live from that childlike place in a very sophisticated, responsible way. And that is at the bottom line of their success. In a way, it reminds me of the movie *Big* in which Tom Hanks plays the role of a small boy who is transformed into an adult man and becomes the vice president of a toy company. With the child at the helm, sales skyrocket!

If companies could harness the imagination and creativity of the three-year-old in their people, they would have no competition. If individuals could find a way to recapture the qualities they had as children, there would be no limit to what they could achieve. Every day would be extraordinary and, to quote the closing line of *Blue's Clues*, "If you use your mind and take a step at a time, you can do anything that you want to do." I hope this book, in some way, touches the child in you so you can realize more of your potential and live a more satisfying life.

CHAPTER 1

Clue In to Your Mission

The *Blue's Clues* Mission: To empower, challenge, and build the self-esteem of preschoolers while making them laugh.

MISSION AS MANTRA

The simple statement above is the guiding light, the foundation, the yardstick, the conscience, and the compass for everyone at *Blue's Clues*. If you could sum up the show's success in one sentence, it would probably be this: They are crystal clear about what their mission is; they are passionate about their mission; and they are vigilant in the ways they live their mission every single day. At *Blue's Clues*, everything begins and ends with the mission. Hardly a decision is made without testing it against the mission. It's a mantra to them, one that they guard with the fierceness of a lioness protecting her cubs.

As you can see from the 8 Secrets to Business Success model in Figure 1.1, the show's mission is at the heart of its success. It informs every decision made, which gives *Blue's Clues* its staying

1

FIGURE 1.1

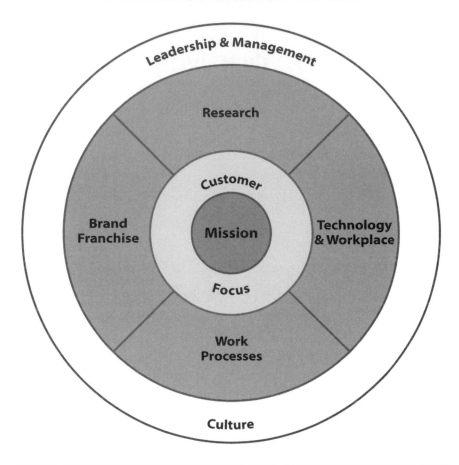

8 Secrets to Business Success

power. It is a phenomenon that has all the signs of becoming an enduring classic. The chapters that follow describe ways people at *Blue's Clues* discipline themselves to be the best at everything they do and how everything they do circles right back to the mission. The clues to their success are all designed to answer the question, How can we empower, challenge, and build the self-esteem of preschoolers while making them laugh?

MANIFESTING THE MISSION

This mission-focused behavior has paid off handsomely for kids, parents, the people who work at *Blue's Clues,* and for the parent company, Nickelodeon. Next to *Rugrats, Blue's Clues* is the most successful children's program ever produced by Nickelodeon. The creators not only created a hit television show—they created the *Blue's Clues* brand, which includes a host of ancillary businesses.

In case you are one who doesn't read book introductions and just in case you have never heard of *Blue's Clues,* it's the savvy, critically acclaimed children's television show for preschoolers. Here are just a few facts that point to how well *Blue's Clues* lives its mission:

- Within the first 18 months of airing, virtually 100 percent of preschoolers' parents knew *Blue's Clues,* an awareness comparable to top-tier programs like *Sesame Street,* a show that has been around for more than 30 years.

- It has one of the highest ratings among all television shows for preschoolers and is the favorite cable preschool program of parents and preschoolers.

- It had the highest rating of any Nickelodeon show premiere.

- Approximately 13.7 million viewers tune in to *Blue's Clues* each week.

- *Blue's Clues* airs in approximately 60 different countries on six continents.

- *Blue's Clues* generated approximately $1 billion in licensing products sold around the world in the year 2000 alone.

- The show has received LIMA (Licensing Industry Manufacturers Association), Prix Jeunesse, Parent's Choice, and many other awards for excellence in children's programming, educational software, and licensing. It has been nominated for nine Emmys.

The

TIPPING POINT

How Little Things Can Make a Big Difference

MALCOLM
GLADWELL

- It was the subject of almost an entire chapter in Malcolm Gladwell's best-selling book, *The Tipping Point,* in which he describes the process through which *Blue's Clues* and other cultural phenomena occur.

- More than ten million *Blue's Clues* books from Simon and Schuster were in print as of Summer 2001.

- The book *Blue's Egg Hunt* made the *New York Times* best-seller list.

- Over the past four years, *Blue's Clues* has been the number-one preschool CD-ROM license. Six *Blue's Clues* CD-ROM titles have sold a total of over three million units since their initial release in 1998.

- Ten *Blue's Clues* video titles have broken the million-unit mark and consistently appear on the top ten on the Children's Video Chart.

- Bathtime Blue, from Fisher-Price was the number-one tub toy for 1999 and 2000.

- In 2001, the Blue's Clues party pattern was the number-one performing Hallmark pattern in Party City, one of the world's largest party-supply superstore chains.

- The 1998 launch of high-quality *Blue's Clues* products at the FAO Schwarz flagship store was the most successful product launch in the 136-year history of the store and was attended by over 7,000 people—in the rain.

That's what can happen when a company really knows its customer, is clear about its mission, and is totally focused on achieving it. But don't think for a minute that they are satisfied with what they have created. They are constantly looking to find new and different ways to please their customers while remaining true to their mission.

Most preschool television programs have about a three-year cycle. *Blue's Clues* has been around since 1996 and looks as though it will be an evergreen property—a classic that will be around for a long time to come. Before I tell you how they developed the powerful mission that propelled them to success, it's important that you know the series of events leading up to their arrival on the preschool television scene in 1996.

SETTING THE STAGE FOR THE MISSION

To fully appreciate *Blue's Clues*'s place in children's television history and how its mission was born, let's go back to 1990 when the state of children's television was pretty dismal. For the most part, Public Broadcasting Service (PBS) was the only source for children's educational programming. Inspired by Peggy Charren, children's television advocate and founder of Action for Children's Television (ACT), Congress passed the Children's Television Act of 1990, which recommended that commercial broadcasters make a reasonable effort to offer educational television to children.

The Act, however, had no teeth, because it didn't specify how much educational television broadcasters had to air, nor did it set criteria or guidelines for what constituted "educational" television. There was no accountability on the part of commercial broadcasters, so nothing changed.

When *Blue's Clues* came on the air in 1996, there was a proliferation of shows for kids, but most of them were violent and designed to sell toys. What commercial broadcasters called "educational" was laughable. Spurred again by ACT, the FCC ruled in 1997 that all commercial broadcasters' (ABC, CBS, NBC, Fox, etc.) affiliates were required to air educational children's television for a weekly minimum of three hours. Any affiliate station that didn't comply would lose its license. The networks began to scramble.

Since Nickelodeon was a cable station, it was not required to meet the commercial broadcasting standard, but they met it anyway—even before it became law. The Nickelodeon mission, which is stated in the form of a "manifesto," demanded it (see Figure 1.2).

Nickelodeon is always looking at the needs of kids and where they can better meet them. They had known for some time that

---

FIGURE 1.2 *The Nickelodeon Manifesto*

Nickelodeon Puts Kids First

1. **Our audience is kids.**
   Nickelodeon is like a club that all kids belong to just because they are kids.

2. **We look at the world from a kid's point of view.**
   When you work for Nickelodeon, it's important to understand what it's like to be a kid.

3. **We invent new stuff for kids.**
   Every time we make something, we make it with our own unique approach.

4. **We are entertaining and safe for kids.**
   Kids and parents can trust Nickelodeon. Nick is a place where kids can be themselves.

5. **We make it kid-tested, kid-approved.**
   Kids are the experts.

---

two- to five-year-olds were being underserved, so they decided to do something about it.

On February 14, 1994, an article appeared on the front page of the *New York Times,* which said that Nickelodeon would invest $60 million in educational television for preschoolers. This was a job for Nick Jr., the Nickelodeon division that develops programming for preschoolers. Led by Executive Vice President Brown Johnson, Nick Jr. set out to be the gold standard for preschool children's programming, a position that had long been held by PBS. One of the things that is unique about Nickelodeon is that they are research fanatics. Nickelodeon does research because they know it is the only way to really know their customer and meet their needs. And their research takes a variety of forms: from formal focus groups, of which they conduct about 250 a year, to their own personal research, which might include a group of executives bringing their favorite childhood games to the office to play with as a way of connecting back to the child within themselves.

Nickelodeon had been producing children's television for years, mostly for the 6- to 12-year age group. Before setting out to improve programming for preschoolers though, they knew they had to do their homework. Nick Jr. called a "summit," which was attended by a diverse group of people from a variety of disciplines: child development experts, toy inventors, a producer from *Mister Rogers' Neighborhood,* teachers, and people who didn't like television at all, to name a few. Nick Jr. posed the question: "What could television be to preschoolers?" Results of that meeting were the seeds for reinventing children's television and a whole new belief system as to television's potential for being a positive influence in the lives of small children. This meeting marked the beginning of a new era in children's television programming.

Prior to this meeting, most people believed that television was a passive medium: it mesmerized and numbed children. It was also believed that children came to television with a blank mind.

Participating in the meeting was child development expert Dan Anderson, a professor from the University of Massachusetts at Amherst, who would eventually come to play a major role in the birth of *Blue's Clues.* Dan Anderson's research indicated the opposite: that preschoolers were mentally active when they watched television. They came to television with an open mind, waiting and wanting to be challenged. From his research he could see that their minds were actually going 100 miles an hour. They were actually thinking, not zoning out while they were watching television.

He also found that preschoolers could and would pay attention for long periods—more than short three- to four-minute segments—if they were told an interesting story by engaging characters. His research showed that kids actually got confused when there were a lot of cuts, a lot of jumping back and forth. With this newfound knowledge, Nickelodeon and Nick Jr. realized they were in a dangerously powerful position with children.

Nick Jr. came away from the meeting with a new mission statement: *To inspire little kids' understanding of the world and themselves through playful entertainment that laughs, sings, and discovers right along with them.* Another important product of the meeting was a new philosophy called "Play to Learn," which guided the creation of *Blue's Clues* as well as every other preschool program developed by Nick Jr. As the famous child psychologist Jean Piaget said: "Play is the natural work of the child." Play has been found to stimulate creativity, grow IQ scores, and facilitate the ability to see things in perspective and language development while improving important social skills such as cooperation and impulse control.

ORIGINS OF THE *BLUE'S CLUES* MISSION

How many times have you had a brilliant idea squashed because a superior couldn't see what you could see, nor did he or she take the time to understand where you were coming from?

One reason companies fail to become phenomenal is because the people of the organization don't trust themselves or each other to entertain way-out ideas—ideas that can become the seeds of greatness if allowed to grow and flourish. Most truly break-through ideas that do come to fruition are initially rejected because they seem so foreign. Thomas Edison, Henry Ford, and Bill Gates are examples of people whose "foreign" ideas changed the world.

One of the unique aspects of the Nickelodeon culture is that it encourages and rewards risk-taking and experimentation. When approached by Brown Johnson of Nick Jr. with the idea of doing a game show for preschoolers, Nickelodeon President Herb Scannell looked at her and asked, "What?" The idea seemed preposterous, but his trust in Johnson was greater than his skepticism about the idea. "Sure, give it a try" was his response.

A game show for preschoolers? What were they thinking? They believed the same things that appeal to adults about game shows would naturally appeal to kids—especially since we know now that preschoolers come to television with an active mind, waiting to be challenged. Think about it: What do viewers like about game shows? They make you think. You get to play along. You feel good when you get the right answer. You are stimulated and challenged and you learn.

But how many answers would a preschooler have? At three or four years of age, your store of knowledge about the world is pretty slim. Granted, it is increasing rapidly every day and it is larger than most adults think, but you still don't know too much. In a world where big people have all the answers and little people are almost totally dependent on them, preschoolers don't have a lot of opportunity to feel smart and powerful. They don't have many opportunities to help others, which would empower them.

What about prizes? Can you just see some kids joyfully skipping away with new toys while others go home empty-handed and crying? And would we want children hollering, screaming, and jumping up and down like the adults they see on television game shows?

Many companies fail to innovate because the people of the organization rule out creative ideas based on assumptions. For example, a game show naturally means that someone wins and someone loses. Innovative, creative thinkers, on the other hand, take an aspect of something familiar, reshape it, reinvent it, and work with it until they come up with something totally different.

The *Blue's Clues* creators took the game-show idea and built upon it. They envisioned a show that would challenge and engage the minds of preschoolers, and invite them to interact with the show and play along with the host. It would help them feel good about themselves when they got the right answer. It would keep their attention by telling a good story.

The creators changed the game-show concept, modified it, and changed the rules to be appropriate for preschoolers. The show would teach cognitive and problem-solving skills. It would also teach social and emotional skills, helping preschoolers understand their own and others' feelings, and modeling peaceful behaviors. It would teach them things like cooperation, sharing, and how to follow directions.

Maybe this is a show adults should be watching. Some do, in fact. Billy Bob Thorton and Angelina Jolie are huge fans of the show and watch it on a regular basis, according to an *US* magazine interview.

THE SPIRITUAL ASPECT

In recent years, a number of books have been written about creating soul in the workplace—probably because it is sorely lacking in most organizations. In general, however, there isn't much talk about the mystical or spiritual aspects of business. This is unfortunate, since these qualities are at the core of the creative process and any lasting business. It's probably why *work* is a four-letter word to many people—why there is no "juice" when they come to work, and why they check their hearts and souls at the door.

Whenever something truly brilliant and out-of-the-box changes the world for the better, there almost always appears to be a mystical or spiritual force working behind the scenes to bring the right people together under the right circumstances. If you have ever been a part of a team that achieved something truly spectacular—maybe it was a sports team, maybe a volunteer group—you know the feeling. There is nothing like it. You are transported to another place and you know the experience won't be easily duplicated. It is not something companies can plan for; they can only create the conditions for it to occur.

Some may call it destiny. Some may attribute it to the stars being in alignment. Others may call it God's will. Still others probably call it luck. Whatever you call it, it's pretty incredible when it happens.

All you have to do is watch a group of preschoolers around a television set to understand the pure joy and excitement *Blue's Clues* brings to them. Or go to the live show at Radio City Music Hall and witness the way the 2,000 kids know every word to every song, and the way they storm the stage to touch the live-action host. In their world, he is no less in stature than Elvis or the Beatles. You realize the people at *Blue's Clues* have touched a central nerve that fosters and encourages all the wonderful qualities of childhood: curiosity, joy, openness, discovery, and learning.

When you get close to that energy, that spirit, you know you are close to something powerful—it's like being in nature and witnessing the miracle of creation. The children's minds are so open, so clear, so innocent. To meet children in that place, as the creators of *Blue's Clues* do, you have to be in touch with that spirit yourself.

So who are these people who conceived this phenomenon? How were they selected? What process did they use to create it? What gave them the inspiration, the confidence? What qualified them to take on such a task? What was it about the people themselves that made it happen?

THE ALIGNING OF THE STARS

Successful teams and companies hire good people and match them to the right job. Those companies that work successfully in teams know all too well how important it is to staff teams with people who have the necessary competencies and experiences.

All too often, however, companies are too rigid in their selection process. Sometimes a talented, "hungry" person with less traditional experience is a better choice than the obvious candidate who is following the usual career track. To tap into the full range of talent within a group, managers must avoid the common trap of judging peoples' potential based on the position they are currently holding. At Nickelodeon, people receive opportunities because they have good ideas and they are passionate, not because they have a particular title or have been with the company for a certain length of time. And this is one of the hallmarks of Nickelodeon's success.

Steve Burns, former actor in the show, credits the *Blue's Clues* creators and producers as the real stars of the show. Steve, who had rock-star status among preschoolers, says, "I get all the benefits and the creators give all the blood, sweat, and tears to make it happen."

The creators of the show—Angela Santomero, Traci Paige Johnson, and Todd Kessler—didn't have the traditional background most children's television producers have, but did possess an amazing combination of talents, backgrounds, and personal attributes. And they were young, which probably worked in their favor. As they have said, "We were too young and naïve to know what we could and couldn't do." Ignorance was bliss.

They were also supported by Nick Jr. and Nickelodeon, both of which were willing to take a risk. They set a few guidelines for the creators and then let them go, something that is common at Nickelodeon but rare in most of corporate America.

Although the young creators didn't have the traditional background, all three had been preparing themselves for what was to become an opportunity of a lifetime. They offer a real lesson in how to achieve career success: prepare, prepare, prepare yourself for the big opportunity, even if you don't know what it will be. Find something you are passionate about and develop your craft. And then watch with the openness of a small child for opportunities to present themselves. And when it appears, seize it with a vengeance.

Angela Santomero did just that. She was working as a researcher for Nick Jr. when she realized a need the organization was looking to fill—the need to create an innovative, breakthrough television program for preschoolers. She didn't wait to be asked to come to the table. She pulled her chair up to the table and asked for the job, which is something women in particular often have difficulty doing.

Although she didn't have traditional production experience, she had something far more powerful: a vision. She had a clear vision of what a game show for preschoolers would look like. This educational show would have all the ingredients of a preschool curriculum and a hands-on approach to learning.

During her postgraduate studies toward a master's degree in developmental psychology with a specialty in instructional technology and media, she read everything she could get her hands on about child development, how children learn, and particularly, the effects of television on children. One of the most poignant studies she came across was one conducted by Dan Anderson, which showed the effects of television violence on kids.

The research on behavior resonance found that when kids walk away from watching television, they feel a certain way. Kids were walking away from violence-based shows with a tendency toward violent behavior.

She became fascinated with the idea that if television could have a powerful negative effect on kids, it could have an equally powerful positive effect on them. She began to ask questions: If we showed characters thinking, would we have a whole nation of kids think-ing more? If we modeled positive self-esteem behav-iors, would that impact their self-esteem? If kids become more vi-olent by watching violent television, then why wouldn't kids be smarter by watching smart television?

Armed with ground-breaking research, a wealth of knowledge about child development and how children learn, and a passion for creating innovative, breakthrough television programming for preschoolers, she presented a proposal for a pilot that would incorporate all her learning about child development and televi-sion, and everything Nick Jr. had learned through extensive work with child development researchers.

Angela was teamed up with Todd Kessler, who was working as a freelance producer at Nick Jr. As a producer and in life in gen-eral, he was always one to challenge the status quo. It was that renegade spirit that helped create something truly breakthrough. They were given $150,000 to create a pilot, a very modest sum as pilots go.

Angela and Todd were ready to create, but they needed an-other creative visionary and rule-breaker who was willing and able to venture outside the boundaries of conventionality to cre-ate something truly breakthrough. Enter Traci Paige Johnson, a young freelancer who had been a designer, cutout animator, writer, producer, and director for children's television.

Traci's example provides wonderful advice for job seekers in today's tough market: Do everything you can to let them know you really want the job, show them you can do the job, and find some unusual way to leave a lasting impression. On her second interview for the job, Traci went to the meeting with ten pages of ideas for games, one of which was called "Help the Pepperoni Find Its Pizza." Perhaps what clinched the job for her was the thank-you note she sent after the interviews in the form of a large, greasy pizza box with a personal note on the back of the box in her own artsy handwriting. They wanted "out-of-the box" and they got it—and the box, too!

Traci had been preparing for her big opportunity for a long time. As early as she can remember, she loved to cut things out of paper. She made cutouts of just about everything. Little did she know that many years later she would use construction paper to change the look of preschool children's television.

In high school, she started producing television programs and fell in love with children's television production at Northwestern University, where she graduated with a degree in radio, television, and film. While she was in college, she created her own unique signature style of cutout animation using construction paper and everyday objects and textures. She probably can best be described as a folk animator.

The stars were aligned. They had the perfect combination of talents and a passion for children's television and had been eagerly waiting for the opportunity to create totally new television programming for preschoolers. They were an all-star team of relative unknowns in the field of children's television production, but they wouldn't be unknown for long.

THE PERSONAL STORY

think almost everything I do, I do from the perspective of a four-year-old. The smallest things make me happy. I love birthdays. I constantly ask "why?"

When I have something to say, I want to be heard and I don't give up easily. I have a new daughter named Hope—through her I realize how much I am still like that small child that I once was.

When I believed we had the best show on television that could educate preschoolers and positively impact their lives, I was relentless. I wanted so much to give kids a television show that celebrates how smart they are, because I truly believe they are brilliant. I also wanted to create a show that would help preschoolers feel good about themselves. It's been proven that the preschool age is the pinnacle of creating the foundation of one's self-esteem. So much of the world's suffering is due to low self-esteem. If a child acquires that foundation, they can face almost anything in life—they will always have hope, because they believe in themselves.

In addition to being determined, like a four-year-old, I fantasize. When we were creating the show, I made up an ending in my mind. I could see it so clearly, even before it happened. I saw a show that people could believe in, that parents would love because it made their jobs easier—a show that would one day become a phenomenon, a classic. Even before we got the funding for the pilot, I had an eye on a dress for the Emmys and I could see the balloon in the Macy's [Thanksgiving] Day Parade. Some thought I was crazy, but the four-year-old in me knew it was all possible.

Angela C. Santomero
Executive Producer and Cocreator

THE BIRTH OF THE *BLUE'S CLUES* MISSION

How many times in your career have you been given the time and freedom to simply create? Most organizations are so task-driven that people rarely have the luxury to create better ways of doing the job. As a result, their creative side atrophies. Granted, the creators of *Blue's Clues* are similar to people in research and development facilities of companies, whose job it is to think up new ideas. Nevertheless, innovating and creating should not be the sole domain of R&D—it should be everyone's responsibility. To fulfill that responsibility though, people must be given the time and resources to do so.

The birthplace of *Blue's Clues* was a small conference room on the 37th floor in the Viacom Building in Times Square, where the three creators locked themselves away for a month to create the show. From this small, glass-surrounded room they could look out onto all of Manhattan—they were literally and figuratively on top of the world.

Virtual strangers to one another when they started, they were about to embark on an experience that would change their lives forever—as well as the lives of millions of preschoolers around the world. They felt as though they were living a dream.

From the first day, the ideas came pouring out. They came from different backgrounds and perspectives, which made their brainstorming rich and intense. They argued, they debated, and they challenged each other, but at the same time, had enormous respect for one another. Each was in a breakthrough frame of mind and was energized by the adrenaline coursing through their bodies. It was their big opportunity and they knew it.

They were having more fun than they had ever had in their lives. It wasn't work, it was sheer ecstasy. They brought endless props to play with: salt and pepper shakers, clocks, and other household items that would eventually become the animated characters in the show.

It was like working with a big ball of unmolded clay that they kept passing around to each other. Each person added his or her own unique contribution, sometimes tearing it apart, until the mission finally manifested itself. While the brainstorming sessions were free-form and free of any judgment, they all agreed that they wanted to create a show that would do the following:

- Incorporate mastery as the key concept as opposed to rote learning or memorization

- Ensure that preschoolers at home know the answer

- Have an element of surprise

- Incorporate what preschoolers like to play

- Be concrete, explicit, and literal in format

- Provide a safe, secure "home base"; the setting would be the world they are most familiar with—the home

- Look like no other show on television

Everyone who works should have at least one mountaintop experience in their careers like the *Blue's Clues* people did. It doesn't have to be on as grand a scale, but when people are given the awesome experience of expressing themselves to the fullest— of using their minds and talents, whatever they may be—they can create something truly extraordinary. If more companies gave people this kind of experience, they would have a lot more committed employees, who look forward to coming to work.

Building on the Best

Sometimes when people try to innovate and create, they throw the baby out with the bathwater. They start with a totally clean slate. Instead, they need to be encouraged to take the best of what they are presently doing and the best of what the competition is doing and improve upon it.

One of the things you will never hear the *Blue's Clues* people do is bash their competition—*Mister Rogers' Neighborhood, Sesame Street,* and *Barney and Friends.* In fact, *Mister Rogers' Neighborhood* was one of the primary inspirations for the show.

Blue's Clues simply took the best aspects of their competition and made it better. If you've ever watched *Mister Rogers' Neighborhood,* for example, you know he speaks at a very slow, measure paced. He's very respectful of his audience. *Blue's Clues* has even more pauses of longer duration than *Mister Rogers' Neighborhood,* because the show's host waits for preschoolers to talk back to him. *Blue's Clues* was built from the ground up to be completely interactive. In fact, the first time parents saw the pilot of *Blue's Clues* before their kids saw it, they thought their kids wouldn't like the show because it was too slow. The live-action host seemed to wait an eternity for the kids to answer. The creators believed that what was an eternity to an adult was a short period for a preschooler who is trying very hard to figure things out at his or her own pace.

How can you improve upon the classic *Sesame Street?* Well, they did. A typical *Sesame Street* show consists of many different segments, none more than three to four minutes. Remember, when *Sesame Street* was created, experts didn't believe preschoolers had the attention span to handle anything other than very short, tightly focused segments. They also didn't believe preschoolers could follow an extended narrative.

Dan Anderson's research and that of others turned that idea on its head, but no one had produced a half-hour narrative for preschoolers to prove it, at least not until *Blue's Clues* came along. The creators also were inspired by Jerome Bruner, a psychologist at New York University who says, "Stories are [children's] way of organizing the world. If they don't catch something in a narrative structure, it doesn't get remembered very well and it doesn't seem to be accessible for further kinds of mulling over."

Sesame Street is quite clever in the way it slips in jokes that are aimed at adults. *Blue's Clues,* on the other hand, made the show perfectly literal without any wordplay or comedy that would confuse preschoolers, one of the many reasons why they show is able to keep children's attention so well.

The *Blue's Clues* creators took the idea of getting kids to interact as they do in *Sesame Street* and *Mister Rogers' Neighborhood* and expanded upon it. From beginning to end, *Blue's Clues* is totally interactive. The live-action host carries on an almost nonstop conversation with the cohosts of the show—the young viewers at home—and they talk back. Preschoolers believe Steve (and now Joe, the new live-action host) hears them when they talk to him.

READY FOR TAKEOFF

The results of Traci, Todd, and Angela's marathon, month-long brainstorm was a formalized mission statement and a pilot that would prove what the creators knew from the very beginning: they were going to the Emmys. They had set out to create a breakthrough show for preschoolers and they knew they had done it. The pilot, originally called *Blue Prints,* was billed as a half-hour "play-a-long, think-a-long" series with the mission to "empower, challenge, and build the self-esteem of preschoolers while making them laugh."

When the pilot was completed, they had created a show for preschoolers that was part game show and part mystery, a cross between *Jeopardy!* and *MacGyver* for little kids. When Nickelodeon President Herb Scannell saw the pilot, he knew they had created something extraordinary that the entire company could get behind, which is exactly what Nickelodeon did.

Unique Elements of the Pilot

So what was it about this pilot that was so different? How did the creators know *Blue's Clues* would become a phenomenon? Here's what set it apart:

- *Blue's Clues* is the first half-hour "think-along" series framed within a narrative structure.

- It is the first series to feature a story driven by the active participation of preschool home viewers.

- The show was and is developed through hands-on work with the real experts on preschool television: preschoolers. More than 100 preschoolers from three to five years of age in day-care centers, preschools, and Head Start programs throughout the New York area contributed to the development of the series.

- *Blue's Clues* is instantly relatable to the preschool audience through the look and feel of its simple, boldly colored storybooks. It was the first children's television show to use desktop computers as the primary tool for producing the show.

- It was the first preschool series to feature a live-action character who "lives" in an animated environment, a fantastical world that preschoolers claim as their own.

Some aspects of the pilot that were, and still are today, critical to the show's success are not as readily apparent. The live-action host, for example, really, really needs the at-home preschooler's help to solve the puzzle or mystery. The viewer is, in fact, a costar of the show. In order for the story to progress, his or her participation is essential.

The friendly, not-quite-adult host is always a step behind the audience, appealing to them for help, which makes them feel very smart. They always get the answer before he does. Research indicates that preschoolers have a keen sense of empowerment due to this important role in the program: "I helped Steve," they say. "He needed me to help him with everything!"

Another example of the not-so-obvious is the cohost, Blue, who is a personable, preverbal, animated puppy. The youngest portion of the preschool audience can especially identify with Blue, who is like them: playful, curious, inquisitive, and a bundle of energy and spirit. Blue never wears a collar or drinks from a bowl, because she is as much preschooler as she is puppy.

THE BIG TEST

Sometimes companies come up with what seems like a great idea, but they don't spend enough time, money, and effort on research—so it never has a chance. One of the most unique aspects of *Blue's Clues* is that the concept for the show was based on lots of research and every episode is researched and tested a minimum of three times during the production. In Chapter 3, you will see just how big a role research plays in the success of *Blue's Clues*.

By the time the creators finished the pilot, they already knew they had a hit, because they had tested it in rough form numerous times before it was completed. Nevertheless, the first time they tested the pilot with preschoolers, the creators were brought to tears by what they saw.

Almost immediately the group of three- to five-year-olds they had assembled to watch the pilot began talking to the live host. As the pilot progressed their excitement grew as they shouted to the host, "over there, look over there, there it is!" as they tried feverishly to help him solve the puzzle. They were responding as the creators had hoped they would respond. It was a breakthrough.

The small viewers also had a physical response to the show. They actually got up out of their seats and ran to the television screen to get closer to the live host, as though they wanted to get inside the television with him. The animated storybook had indeed come to life for them in a very real way.

The pilot also totally captivated their attention and sustained it through the entire length of the show, another breakthrough. At that point, there was no doubt in the creators' minds that they had created a phenomenon.

THE CHALLENGE

As you can see, an enormous amount of research, critical thinking, and creativity went into the making of *Blue's Clues*. The creators knew they had a mega-hit and the president of Nickelodeon gave it his support, but how would they convince others within the company of its potential? There were those who got it and those who didn't. Some were skeptical because the show was so different from anything else on the air, and others were skeptical because the three creators had no other children's television productions under their belts.

Sometimes creators of television shows hit on a good idea and it takes off. In this case, it was a matter of conscious competence—the creators of the show knew exactly what they were doing and why the show was destined to become a phenomenon. It was that knowing or competence that gave them the confidence and gusto to persevere in their quest to ensure the show's rightful place in preschool television history. Nevertheless, they had a challenge: to sell people on the concept of the pilot and translate the mission to all other aspects of the business.

SELLING THE CONCEPT AND TRANSLATING THE MISSION

Sometimes great ideas die an early death because people don't know how to market and sell the ideas. The creators of the idea spend little or no time helping the rest of the company see what they see. Without a shared vision, there is nothing on which people can focus their efforts—nothing that excites and calls forth the best in them.

How they translated the mission and vision to every part of the *Blue's Clues* business is the subject of the rest of this book. One of the things they did though from the beginning was to use the power of suggestion. They planted seeds. They consistently used words and phrases within the company—such as "signature show for Nick Jr.," "*Blue's Clues* is a phenomenon," "*Blue's Clues* is breakthrough"—before it became any of those things in the minds of the audience. The creators knew it and they claimed it!

They put the *Blue's Clues* signature—Blue's paw print—on just about everything they did. And they started talking about branding before it had become a catchy business buzzword. But here's where they were really smart: They thought of every person or department in the company whose support they knew they would need in order to become the phenomenon they knew they already were. They worked relentlessly to help them understand *Blue's Clues* and how it could serve the other person or department's objectives. They learned to work their way through the Nickelodeon system. They knew creativity was not enough; they needed to have savvy people skills to make the show a hit. They had to empower, challenge, and in some ways, build the self-esteem of everyone with whom they came in contact in order to fulfill their mission.

CLUES FOR Creating a Mission for Your Organization

Many companies have mission statements on plaques and pieces of paper; too few have them inscribed on the hearts and minds of the people whose job it is to actualize the mission. If you ask most people to recite the mission statement for their company, department, or team, they would be hard-pressed to do so.

To Whom It May Concern:

A couple of months ago, my 23-month-old son was a terror. He would not go to sleep before 1 AM. He had no kind of schedule. I felt like a failure as a mother. There just wasn't a way to get my child on a schedule. I had tried everything—or at least I thought I had.

Then one morning I turned on *Blue's Clues* while I cleaned house. Over the next week, Chase began to calm down and get on a schedule. He began going to sleep at a decent hour and got up early enough to watch *Blue's Clues*. In the past two months we have bought *Blue's Clues* books, movies, playhouses, extra characters, and a pose of Blue. He just loves watching the show.

Two months ago we were trying to make appointments with an ear doctor and speech therapist because we were convinced he had impaired hearing. A couple of weeks after watching the show and now he listens to directions and is actually speaking words we can understand. I just wanted to thank everyone at *Blue's Clues* for helping me and my son. A miracle has happened with the creation of this show.

Your Biggest Fan,
Ashly Nickols-Hutson

The result? People go to work as task-oriented, rote performers instead of vision-oriented, creative thinkers and problem solvers. Companies everywhere lose an enormous amount of productivity and innovation for one simple reason: They don't give their people anything meaningful to care about.

Developing an effective mission statement is the first step. Getting people to own and commit to it is the second step. In Chapter 7, we will address the subject of how to keep people focused on and connected to the mission so they have meaning and direction in their jobs. Here are some questions to help you check the quality of your mission statement if you already have one:

- Does it clearly define why we exist?

- Can people remember it easily?

- Do people feel good when they read it? Does it inspire?

- Does it provide a good framework for decision making?

- Does it define how we are different?

- Does it reflect what we value?

If you don't have a mission statement, here are some steps you can use to create one:

- Involve as many people in the organization as possible in the development of the mission statement.

- If the original founders of the company or group are around, ask them what they were thinking and feeling when they founded it.

- Ask people within the company to speak from the heart about what makes them proud about the company.

- Encourage people to think about what they would like the company to be if it isn't that already.

- Ask people to tell stories from their own personal experience that reflect the impact their product or service has on customers and the world.

- Ask people to think about what makes the company or team unique.

Involving everyone in the creation of a mission statement can be time-consuming, but it is the best way to get true ownership and commitment. By getting people to reflect and talk about what they think and feel about the company, the following happens:

- People feel that they count, that someone cares about what they are thinking.

- While they are reflecting and creating, they are internalizing the good things about the company.

- People begin to make connections between what they do in their jobs and the company's larger purpose.

- Management gets a richness of ideas and a better understanding of how people feel about the company.

SUGGESTED EXERCISE

One way to get people excited about the idea of developing a mission statement is by letting them express themselves through art. It works best when you divide people into small groups of four to six people, give each group a big bag of art supplies, and ask them to express through art what they think is the company, team, or department's mission. Encourage them to be as creative as possible.

You will be amazed by what people will create. The exercise creates a spirit of collaboration and teamwork. By owning their artwork, people in some way own the mission. People get out of their heads and into their feelings, which is an essential step to getting ownership and commitment. If people don't feel it, they won't own it.

CLUES FOR Finding Your Own Life's Mission

When we are young, we dream of all the great things we are going to be when we grow up. Our minds have yet to be poisoned by well-meaning caregivers and society in general who give us messages such as we can't, we aren't smart enough, we aren't good enough. Because we can't distinguish between what is real and what is not real when we are small, the bogus ideas become a part of our belief system from which we create our life experience. Most people settle for so little, set their sights too low, and die with all their greatness still within them. But it's never too late. You can change it as long as you are still breathing.

The first step to finding your mission in life—finding that job or career that sets your soul on fire—is to examine and change your belief system. It's not easy work, but it is the most important work you will ever do. Once you break through the barrier of your own self-limiting beliefs, anything is possible. When you believe you have a destiny, that you are put on Earth for a reason, that you have greatness within you that the world needs, your search to find your life's mission becomes a very different experience. Instead of half-heartedly wishing and hoping that there's something meaningful out there for you, you know it is out there—all you have to do is find it.

At some point in life we have to make a decision: We are either going to take the path of least resistance or we are going to dream big and work to make the dream come true. As Helen

Keller said, "Life is either a daring adventure or nothing." Let's say you have made the decision to find your life's calling. How do you find it? Many people say, "I would go for it if I only knew what *it* was. Here are some suggestions for finding your mission in life:

Commit yourself totally. You have to think of finding your life's mission as a job in itself. No matter how difficult or how impossible it may seem in the beginning, you must resolve to stick with it. Everytime you get knocked down by the ghost beliefs about yourself—those limiting beliefs that simply aren't true—or someone tries to tell you it's impossible, or life deals you a disappointment, you have to pick yourself up and keep going. You must believe that you will find it. And you will.

Resurrect your childhood dreams. Sometimes the dreams we had when we were a child are the keys to what we want to do or be today—we just forgot them. What did you want to be when you were a child and why? Try to recall what those experiences and dreams felt like. What activities had special meaning for you when you were little?

Talk to people who know you. Sometimes other people can recognize our talents and gifts better than we can. Talk to the people in your life who know you and support you. Ask them what they think your strengths and gifts are. Tell them you are doing an inventory of your talents and abilities and would like their objective opinion. (This is not a time to be modest—you are trying to mine your good stuff.)

Look at the patterns of your life. When you look back over your life, what are the recurring themes? What are the tasks or activities you constantly find yourself doing—at work and outside of work? Are you the organizer? Are you the nurturer? Are you the writer? What comes naturally and easy to you?

Look to your life challenges for clues. Sometimes the gifts we have to give the world are born out of hardships, weaknesses, and struggles. Christopher Reeve and his mission to find a cure for spinal cord injuries is a perfect example. James Earl Jones is another—he stuttered badly when he was young, yet he became a famous actor.

Do an inventory of your skills. When you look at your skills, make a list of the things you know: What is your knowledge base? What are you an expert in? (Don't worry if you don't have an area of expertise right now.) Make a list of the things you can *do,* as well as the skills you have in working with people: negotiating, supervising, communicating, and so on.

Make a list of your values. What do you care passionately about? Make a list of the times in your life when you were involved in something that gave you pure joy—when you wanted the experience to last forever. What were those experiences when you had a deep-down feeling of fulfillment, when you felt really alive?

As you go through these thought processes, don't limit yourself in any way. Every time your mind starts to wander down a certain path and your mind tells you things like, "You can't do that because you don't have enough education" or "You can't do that because you have responsibilities," *stop.* Don't limit your thinking in any way. First you have to learn to dream again. We aren't trying to figure out *how* you are going to fulfill your life's dream, we are trying to find out *what* it is. The how will come later.

SUGGESTED EXERCISE

Find a quiet, peaceful spot where you can be alone for a good block of time. If you have a special place where you go to get inspired, go there. Bring a pad of paper and a pen with you. After you have answered the previous questions, put your responses aside and let yourself dream. Begin by writing the story of your life. We all have a story and within that story is our life's mission. It may not be apparent to you, but it is there. Start way back when you were very young. Walk yourself through the phases of your life—what were your dreams then, what were you feeling, what were the events that shaped your life?

When you get to the present, let your mind go. Finish the story. What would be the perfect ending to your life? What will you have accomplished? What will you have said to the world? How will the world be better because of your life?

CHAPTER Summary

The mission of an organization should be so clear and focused that anyone reading it can understand instantly what the company does and why it exists. Having a clear mission statement on paper, however, is not enough. The leaders must bring it to life and inspire the people of the organization to own it. Everyone must be trained to use the mission as the basis for every decision he or she makes.

In order for a business to become a phenomenon, it must have a mission that meets a need for customers in a new and powerful way. The mission should engage the hearts and minds of the people who are charged with executing it. The more the mission provides people with a sense of mission and purpose for their own lives, the more the company will be able to harness the potential of the people who work for the company.

Clue #1

A clear and powerful *mission* provides the focus for mobilizing the energy of your people. If it is one they can believe in, you can win their hearts as well as their minds, which is essential to your business success.

CHAPTER 2

Clue In to Your Customer

THE *BLUE'S CLUES* CUSTOMER REIGNS

Just imagine what kind of world this would be if every company from which you bought a product or service really did treat you as if you were someone special, if every company you patronized stayed totally focused on how it could please and delight you; how it could help you feel better about yourself and more empowered; how it could make your life easier and more meaningful.

Well that's exactly what they do at *Blue's Clues*. It is one of the many secrets behind their success. In order to fulfill their mission to empower, challenge, and build the self-esteem of preschoolers while making them laugh, they know they must stay totally focused on their customer. And who is their customer? Two- to five-year-olds. Parents and caregivers are customers, too, but they are secondary. At *Blue's Clues,* preschoolers reign supreme. Every decision is made with them in mind. And almost every major decision is preceded by an enormous amount of research.

Companies large and small can learn a powerful lesson from *Blue's Clues:* Know thy customer, listen to thy customer, love thy customer, and make him or her the focus of everything you do. Think of the amount of money spent in this country on sophisticated advertising and marketing campaigns that don't work, campaigns that make promises companies all too often fail to keep. That's probably why most of us have become immune to advertising, why the "mute" button on the television remote gets so much use. And think of the number of companies that have lost substantial amounts of market share after years of phenomenal success, all because they did not listen to their customers. They made the dangerous assumption that the world would stay the way it was and that they knew what their customers wanted.

NO EGOS ALLOWED

Most companies start out wanting to please the customer but this desire gets lost for one reason or another. People, for example, get so immersed in their own work and their own creative processes that they forget for whom they are creating. For people who have little or no customer contact, the customer is often in the background of their thinking process.

Everything at *Blue's Clues,* however, is about the customer. It's about educating them and making them feel smart, making things funny, making them laugh, making them feel loved.

If the kids don't understand something or lose interest when researchers test a script, the creators don't get bent out of shape because the kids thumbed their nose at their magnificent, creative work. They try to understand why it didn't work, which enables them to make not just a change, but the correct change. Pride of authorship is a luxury creators, producers, writers, and animators know they cannot afford if they are going to serve their customer well.

How many times have you been inconvenienced as a customer because the company had policies and procedures that made no sense whatsoever? They seem to be designed to make your life miserable. In your own career experience, how often have you seen managers make decisions designed to either line their pockets or put themselves in a positive light at the expense of the customer?

At *Blue's Clues,* they don't develop timetables, processes, or formulas that make things easy for the people who work at the production company while hurting the customer or product. And decisions are never made by managers whose primary mission is to promote their own self-interests. If you work at *Blue's Clues,* it's almost a sacred trust. It's understood by all that everything they do is for the kids.

The skeptic in you may be thinking, "Sure they stay focused on their customer so they can sell more advertising and move more consumer products—it's all about money." The truth is, the creators and producers of *Blue's Clues* as well as the people at Nickelodeon and Nick Jr. really do love kids. They are a profit-making business that has done extremely well because they put kids first. In fact, *Blue's Clues* was the first commercial television program for preschoolers that was educational and profitable. They proved that "good for kids" and "profitability" are not mutually exclusive notions—they are, in fact, closely linked.

Blue's Clues has spawned a variety of ancillary businesses that are quite profitable. Each one was developed around the needs and best interests of preschoolers. Preschoolers, for example, play with toys, so their philosophy was to develop the best educational toys possible—toys that would meet the same high educational and entertaining standards as the show.

Blue's Clues is such an unusual work environment that you almost have to see it to believe it. As you walk down the brightly decorated corridors of the *Blue's Clues* studios, you see talented young adults—some 85 of them—working diligently to create joy and happiness for two- to five-year-olds. It's a sweet sight. It reminds one of a big brother or big sister getting a kick out of taking a much younger sibling on a magnificent, exciting adventure, all because they love them. In the process, they get to be kids again, too.

Most business books don't talk much about love, but we have to talk about it here because it is the driving force behind the customer focus of *Blue's Clues*. As artists, they have strong egos—they have to in order to do the work that they do. But their egos are in service of their love for children, which means decisions are almost always made for the right reasons.

At most companies, people either avoid conflict because they think it is dangerous or they are overly confrontational for the wrong reasons. At *Blue's Clues,* they aren't afraid to argue, debate, and challenge one another for the sake of their customer. They don't mince words or try to preserve one another's feelings at the expense of their customers. The people at *Blue's Clues* accept and welcome that kind of direct confrontation and communication from one another because they know it's coming from a good place: the mission. And when feelings do get hurt, as they do from time to time, they discuss it, work through it, and get over it. Their focus on the mission brings them back. It's the glue that keeps the team together.

It's always interesting when *Blue's Clues* business partners go to the *Blue's Clues* offices for a meeting for the first time. Seasoned, high-level executives from companies such as Hallmark, Fisher-Price, Kraft, and Paramount Studios think they are coming to just another business meeting. When they arrive, they are blown away. They have never experienced anything like it. They feel the passion and the love. They see the brilliant creative work in execution. They witness the singleness of motive with which everything is done. They usually leave scratching their heads, wondering, "How do these people do it?" It looks like pure magic.

BEHIND THE MAGIC

Like a professional ballet dancer or opera singer, the leaders at *Blue's Clues* make it look easy. But behind the magic is a lot of thought, planning, and hard work. Getting that kind of commitment from people, keeping them focused and marching in the same direction, and giving them an extraordinary work experience don't just happen. And it isn't so much a factor of the nature of the product, which is fun and educational. The leaders at *Blue's Clues* take just as much care in creating the culture of the company as they take in creating the show. It's one of the things that separates them from the pack. They are wise beyond their years. They apply their mission to their employees as well as their customers— you could say they empower, challenge, and build the self-esteem of their employees while giving them a good time at work.

In Chapters 7 and 8, we will talk more about the *Blue's Clues* culture, what makes it so special, how they are able to tame the ego in everyone for the sake of the mission, and how they make winners out of everyone. But first, here are some ways they keep the customer at the center of everything they do.

FEATURES AND FORMAT OF THE SHOW

Like every other aspect of the show and its ancillary businesses, the features and format of *Blue's Clues* are based on a wealth of research, as you will see in the next chapter. Like any product or service designer, they asked themselves questions such as: What needs are currently not being met for our customer? What are the primary benefits we want to give our customers? What is it specifically that we want this show to do for them? Here's what they came up with: a format that would allow the show to do the following:

- Teach preschoolers kindergarten readiness skills by using a thinking skills curriculum presented in a play-to-learn, game-like fashion.

- Empower preschoolers to learn through active participation in activities that are increasingly challenging, developmentally appropriate, and grounded in their everyday lives. By doing so, preschoolers would be better able to master concepts on their own.

- Provide preschoolers with opportunities for problem solving in an environment that engages them to think, laugh, and feel good about themselves.

- Enable preschoolers, parents, teachers, and caregivers to extend and transfer the learning experiences and thinking skills utilized in the show to their everyday lives.

- Foster the social development of preschoolers through the natural interaction among all the characters as well as the interaction between the two main characters and the home audience.

The challenge was how to achieve these ambitious goals in the format of a 30-minute show that would be both educational and entertaining. Here are some of the features and benefits of the show that demonstrate the *Blue's Clues* customer focus:

Learning in the context of everyday life. Preschoolers are like sponges; they learn from everything they do. Children and adults alike learn better when concepts are made relevant to their lives. By situating the learning in a safe, secure environment with which they are familiar—the home—the show is able to deliver the following benefits: *attention, comprehension, and learning.*

Active participation. The preschooler is an integral part of the continuation of the story. The host looks at the audience, asks a question, pauses for a response, and then positively reinforces what the audience has "said." Because preschoolers are egocentric, each child at home thinks the host is talking directly to him or her. By responding to the host, the preschooler actually owns the information. *The benefits are empowerment, enhanced learning and memory, motivation, and self-esteem building.*

Multilayering. *Blue's Clues* is layered visually and developmentally to increase the challenge the concept taught as the episode progresses. The show is designed to appeal to kids in the entire two to five target age group, no small feat when you consider the developmental differences within this group and how fast kids develop at these ages. Incorporated into the format of each episode are a number of different layers: solving the *Blue's Clues* puzzle, which requires abstract and critical thinking to make inferences about the answer, is designed for the five-year-olds, while finding the clues uses visual discrimination skills that are more developmentally suited for the younger segment of the audience.

In addition, concepts and information are scaffolded. *Scaffolding* is an instructional principle that helps promote the mastery of concepts. It involves guiding the learner through a series of trials that allow them to succeed. *The benefits are mastery, attention, and motivation.*

Multiple viewing. Each *Blue's Clues* episode airs five consecutive days in a week, something that was previously unheard of in children's television. Because the show has so many layers of learning, kids can watch the same episode over and over and not get bored. Children naturally repeat behaviors when they are learning—just like they want to watch the same video or read the same book over and over. *The benefits are learning and mastery.*

Challenge and mastery. *Blue's Clues* never underestimates the audience's ability to learn concepts. The show challenges audience members by exposing them to complex topics in a way that is preschool-appropriate. *The benefit is a stronger foundation for future learning, which can impact them the rest of their lives.*

Modeling. Television is a powerful medium, and preschoolers are prone to imitating behaviors that they see—that's how they learn and master their world. The show is careful to never show anything that is not appropriate for preschoolers to mimic. *The benefit is responsible behavior.*

Structure. The show is structured to give preschoolers a feeling of comfort and predictability. Every episode begins the same and certain things happen in every episode like the singing of the "Mail Song" when the mail arrives. It's something they can look forward to because they know it's coming and they have mastered it. *The benefits are comfort and participation.*

Mnemonics. Many episodes use memory devices such as mantras and songs to repeat a message that they want preschoolers to walk away with and hopefully use in their everyday lives. One such song is the "Planets Song," which has taught many children and adults the planets, their attributes, and where they are in relation to the sun. *The benefits are learning, memory, and the ability to generalize.*

Metacognitive wrap-up. This is a fancy term for the process of reinforcing what someone knows. At the end of every episode, Blue and the host celebrate the solution to *Blue's Clues* and in doing so, rehearse and recap the ideas or concepts they learned throughout the episode. *The benefits: learning and self-esteem.*

DESIGN AND LOOK OF THE SHOW

Have you ever bought a new car or piece of furniture that you absolutely fell in love with because the look was so stunning? The design couldn't have been better if you had designed it yourself.

The look of the show was designed to make preschoolers fall in love with *Blue's Clues*. A team of talented artists work hard to make it look as though preschoolers had a hand in designing it. Getting that to happen was a huge undertaking.

When Traci Paige Johnson, one of the original creators introduced in Chapter 1, designed the look of *Blue's Clues*, she had no process to follow. Like Angela Santomero, she had a vision of what the show would look and feel like, but nothing on television for preschoolers looked remotely like what she had in mind. She was going to have to travel into unchartered waters and create something completely new.

To create a look that would facilitate the goals of the show and appeal to preschoolers, Traci reached back into her own experience as a child. She took all the things she loved as a preschooler and translated them into the visuals and designs that give the show its unique, out-of-the-box look today.

She wanted the show to look and feel safe and warm to preschoolers. She wanted it to spark and engage them. At the same time, she wanted it to feel soothing and peaceful. As mentioned in Chapter 1, Traci has loved cutting things out of construction paper since she was a child. In college, she created the cutout style used in the show today. She used simple cutouts to create a graphic storybook that would be so "yummy" (a word that is used frequently at *Blue's Clues*) that kids would want to reach out and touch it.

Blue's Clues was the first cutout animation series for preschoolers. Instead of using animated puppets and bombarding the audience with wacky colors and sets like most television shows for preschoolers, *Blue's Clues* introduced them to a world of soothing colors and environments and simple animation.

Traci even called upon her preschool self in designing the color schemes. The color schemes actually come from her love as a preschooler of going into art stores where all the colors are organized into groups. If you look closely, you'll see that each room in the show has a certain color organization. And the green striped shirt worn by the former host, Steve—did it remind you of anything? Traci loved Fruit Stripe gum as a child.

One of the main style goals was to make *Blue's Clues* feel *"organic"* (another *Blue's Clues* buzzword). They wanted it to feel as natural as possible. The show shouldn't look like it was created in a computer. There would be no "computery" designs or animations. They wanted it to look as though it had been freshly

Blue's Clues "organic" look is achieved with three-dimension objects created by the Art and Design department, shown here by Ian Chernichaw, senior art director for *Blue's Clues*. (photo by Gallucci Imaging, Inc.)

cut and glued together with a vivid array of textures, colors, and shadows.

Simplicity was the other main style goal. Less is more, especially with two- to five-year-olds. All of the elements use simple cutout shapes with no complicated lines or details. Research has shown that preschoolers embrace this pared-down style, which is reminiscent of childhood picture book illustrations or felt boards.

At the same time, they sprinkle three-dimensional objects throughout the show. They actually build real-life miniatures. For example, with a birthday cake, instead of cutting it out of paper which has a flat look, the art and design department creates a birthday cake out of clay and shoots it with a camera. The digital design department then cuts it out and places it into the background. This way, the objects look very real and the live host looks perfectly at home in the environment.

"Storybook animation" is another buzzword at *Blue's Clues*. It describes the show's unique design style. Essentially, they animate in a two-dimensional environment, like in the pages of a book but using three-dimensional elements that add perspective and depth. The result is a magical storybook come to life.

THE PERSONAL STORY

I think we are all born creative, but some of us lose it along the way. I was fortunate to have a mother who took as much care in nourishing my young creative nature as she took in feeding and clothing me.

There were boundaries for my behavior but virtually none when I was expressing my creative self. If I wanted to draw on tin foil with magic markers, that was fine. If I wanted to wear a hat in the bathtub as I belted out a tune in my own one-woman show, that was fine. If I wanted to build stuff with checkers instead of playing *checkers, that was fine, too. She always encouraged me to "color outside the lines." My self-expression was celebrated but never judged.*

What's amazing to me is that when I was little, I never dreamed that the bag of paper scraps—wallpaper, wrapping paper, construction paper, etc.—that was always around for me to play with, actually held my destiny as an artist. The construction paper cutouts I made as a child from those scraps were the seeds for the design of the show. What's even more amazing—or maybe it's not—I never went to art school or animation school. Who knows? If I had, I may not have gotten the job. I think Nickelodeon hired me because my art was fresh and different; because I broke the rules and looked at the world in a quirky, different way.

Creativity is such a wonderful thing. For me it's about being fully alive. It's about expressing what's deep down inside you. It's about saying something to the world in a way that only you can say it. As a young mother myself, I am trying very hard to give my son T.J. the same creative freedom I had as a child—the very same freedom we try to encourage on Blue's Clues.

Traci Paige Johnson
Executive Producer, Design Director, and Cocreator

TELEVISION HOST CASTING

Have you ever seen a really good movie but the casting just didn't work? The story line was great, but one or more of the characters either weren't believable or didn't connect with the other character or characters. When the *Blue's Clues* creators cast the live actor who hosted the show, they were not about to let that happen.

The casting of the television show's live host is one more example of how the creators stay focused on their customer. So many elements contribute to the phenomenal success of *Blue's Clues,* but none is more important than the live actor. Finding the perfect actor would prove to be a monumental task.

The person had to be the translator and embodiment of the creator's vision. The actor had to be able to empower, challenge, and build the self-esteem of preschoolers while making them laugh. He or she had to be someone parents could trust but more important, someone the kids would love—someone on the order of a great camp counselor, the preschool teacher kids adore, or the babysitter they can't wait to see again—someone who wasn't afraid to get down on the floor and play with kids.

The television actor needed to be someone who could talk convincingly and directly to the camera and elicit interaction from the kids. The eyes, the facial expressions, the gestures, the pacing—all were essential to establishing a strong connection with the kids. One of the things that makes the job challenging is that the actor is shot in front of nothing but a big blue background, which is later removed. There's nothing for the actor to interact with or play off of. All the characters and the *Blue's Clues* world are added later, when the show is animated on desktop computer.

As always, the creators looked to research to find out what personal characteristics in a television host are most effective with young children. Dan Anderson's research found that children would be more attentive to a female host, because female hosts tend to have more variance in their vocal tones and they gesture more. They also usually speak more slowly, smile more, and are more approachable than their male counterparts.

With this knowledge, the creators set out to find the perfect host. Of the hundreds of actors and actresses who auditioned for the part, the creators immediately knew who was their favorite, but it was not a woman. It was a 21-year-old actor named Steve Burns who had just moved to New York from Boyerstown, Pennsylvania. He had all the characteristics they were looking for, but he had something much more. During the audition, from the time the cameras started rolling, he was there—he was *in* the creators' *Blue's Clues* world. He immediately brought it to life. It was like watching a child playing pretend when he crosses over the line from pretending to believing.

What was particularly amazing was that the pilot had not even been created at this point. He was working off nothing but a blue screen with absolutely no animation. It was as though he could see everything just as it was in the minds of the creators: the characters, the scenes, everything.

He also made the connection. The creators were watching the audition on a television screen to see if he could connect through the television, and he did. To this day, they still don't know how he gave such a superb, on-target performance with so little information. They later learned that when he showed up for the audition he thought he was auditioning for a voice-over part.

The creators were sold, but they were not the ones who had to be sold—the audience had to be sold. When they showed the two callback tapes (the other finalist was a woman) to a group of preschoolers, there was no contest. The kids immediately started screaming, pointing, and talking back to Steve, which is pretty amazing when you consider there was no animation—just Steve and a few props. He was destined for the part.

The creators had broken another rule: the host would be a male instead of a female as the research recommended. That meant the puppy, Blue, would be a female—another rule broken. As Steve Burns grew the character, he too broke rules. He is anything but your typical children's television host. There is nothing syrupy about him—his humor is sometimes borderline offbeat, but never inappropriate for preschoolers. Like everyone who is associated with *Blue's Clues*, he respects preschoolers and believes they are much smarter than most people think, and it comes across in the show.

When Steve Burns decided to leave the show and move on in his career as an actor, his character, Steve, was embedded in the psyches of two- to five-year-olds everywhere. What would they do without their Steve? Could he ever be replaced? The answer is yes and no.

While the *Blue's Clues* creators wished Steve well and were very grateful to him for all the wonderful contributions he had made to the show, they were concerned. They didn't want to disappoint a nation of preschoolers. They had to find another host who would be equally as wonderful, and they had to explain Steve's departure to preschoolers in a way that they could understand and accept.

Instead of having Steve disappear all at once, the creators carefully developed a three-episode transition that was heavily re-searched and tested with preschoolers before it aired. In the first two episodes, the kids and parents are introduced to Steve's younger brother, Joe. They get to know him, play with him, and trust him in the first two episodes and in the third episode they learn that Steve is going off to college and that Blue and the rest of the *Blue's Clues* characters are going to stay with Joe.

This time, the creators auditioned thousands of actors, most of whom left them cold because they tried to imitate Steve, which just didn't work. And then one day, a young actor by the name of Donovan Patton came in to audition for the part. Once again, they knew he was the one. Interestingly, Donovan had never seen *Blue's Clues* when he auditioned for the part. He and Steve were different, but they had one major thing in common: imagination. Like Steve, Donovan was able to magically bring the characters and the *Blue's Clues* world to life.

Steve will always have a special place in the hearts of pre-schoolers—he can't be replaced. But now preschoolers have a new friend who is equally wonderful. Joe has some of the same fea-tures as Steve, but he is his own person—Steve's younger, hipper, sillier, much taller brother. Oh, and the kid's test of Donovan? He passed with flying colors. They responded just as enthusiastically to Donovan's callback tape as they did to Steve's. Besides having a new friend, it's a lesson learned for preschoolers: Life changes, people move on, and it's okay.

When I took on the role of "Steve" (yes that's my real name), I never dreamed I would be a part of something that would have such a powerful influence on so many children. In the beginning it was just a job, but it wasn't long before it became something different.

The moments when I fully realized the importance of the work I was doing are etched in my memory forever—like riding in the Macy's Thanksgiving Day Parade with the huge Blue balloon towering overhead. Tens of thousands of kids were waving ecstatically, shouting my name, so excited to see in person the Steve from the show they love. Some of them were even dressed like me in their green striped shirts.

Some of my best memories are those with children and families who had requested a visit from me through the Make-a-Wish Foundation. I traveled the country visiting critically ill children whose one wish was to meet "Steve." There are no words to explain how it feels to know that you can bring so much joy to a sick child who is bravely fighting a difficult battle. I don't know who benefited most from our time together—them or me.

And then there were the scores of letters and e-mails I received from the parents of autistic children and other kids who were speech-delayed. The parents were convinced that Blue's Clues *had wrought miracles where conventional treatment methods had failed. It is just one of the many testaments to the power of the television medium and the brilliance of* Blue's Clues.

One of the wonderful things about being "Steve" was that I got to live in the fantastical world of the two- to five-year-old and I got to play. That is why I know my replacement, Donovan Patton, will do a wonderful job as "Joe" on the show. He has the true heart of a child and a playful spirit like no other adult I have ever met.

I am proud to say that I helped select Donovan. His audition was very impressive, but there was something else that told me he was it. At some time during

MACY'S THANKSGIVING DAY PARADE: © 2002 Macy's East, Inc. A sub-
sidiary of Federated Department Stores. All Rights Reserved.

callbacks he came to the office with his five-year-old little sister. The way he re-lated to her was something beautiful. Offscreen he knew how to enter the world of a child, so I knew he had it in him to do it on the show.

I am forever indebted to the creators of Blue's Clues *for allowing me the op-portunity to be a part of children's television history. I will miss them and all the* Blue's Clues *characters, and I wish Donovan as many good times and magical moments as I had.*

Steve Burns

BLUE'S CLUES MUSIC

Like every other aspect of the show, the music was created to meet the special needs and interests of preschoolers, but not in the way one might think. The music is preschool-appropriate but it is in no way characteristic of the music you hear in most children's television shows. For one, if you close you eyes and listen to the music, you will think you are listening to music for adults.

From the beginning, the creators of *Blue's Clues* knew they wanted music that would be different. They wanted an organic, natural sound and wanted to expose kids to all kinds of music. They wanted to underscore the show almost exclusively using live musicians instead of synthesizers.

They searched for quite some time for musicians who could create the music they had in mind. Michael Rubin, composer and owner of Murmur Music production studio in New York City, and Nick Balaban, a composer and pianist, were destined to be a part of the line-up of stars who worked behind the scenes to actualize the creators' vision of creating a breakthrough television show that challenged and respected young children.

Not only were they talented musicians, composers, and producers, they too were visionaries. Upon viewing the pilot, they knew they had a unique opportunity—one that had never been available to Mike in all the years he had been producing advertising for clients such as AT&T, Nabisco, General Motors, and Samsung. It also was a unique opportunity for Nick, who was accustomed to composing and playing primarily for adults.

Their thinking was this: By the time children are age six or seven, their musical tastes have already been influenced by older siblings and adults. But two- to five-year-olds? Their minds are wide open. Why not use that small window of time in their development to expose them to as many different styles of music and as many different instruments as possible? Who knows what could come from a child's early exposure to a variety of musical sounds?

Mike and Nick, like the *Blue's Clues* creators, believed that preschoolers were far brighter than most people give them credit for and are capable of enjoying many of the same things adults enjoy. To Mike, his two young sons were living examples of this. Every time he put on Macedonian brass band music in his home, they would run around the room in sheer ecstasy.

In addition to exposing the audience to a variety of different kinds of music, Mike and Nick recommended that live musicians create the music—it was the only way to get the organic sound the creators had been searching for.

One of the show's goals is to empower preschoolers, and the music does just that. It helps carry the show's emotional through line and provides a sense of playfulness, a sense of joy, and a sense of the fantastic, boundlessness of imagination. *Blue's Clues* is a very "soulful" television show. When you consider that music is the language of the soul for kids as well as adults, Mike and Nick's contribution to the show's success as well as the success of the videos, CDs, and live show is enormous.

In the past two years, Mike and Nick have created original music for more than 100 *Blue's Clues* episodes, presenting kids with a multitude of different musical styles including jazz, country, bluegrass, R&B, funk, disco, classical, gospel, doo-wop, Dixieland, blues, bossa nova, rockabilly, reggae, bebop, African kora, French impressionist, klezmer, and a host of others.

Although Mike and Nick want the music to be live, they also want it to be simple, so they bring musicians into the studio one or two at a time. In addition to exposing children to different styles of music, they also have introduced them to a variety of instruments: piano, organ, accordion, guitar, French horn, trumpet, cornet, saxophone, oboe, bassoon, English horn, violin, viola, cello, harp, drums and other percussion instruments, musical saw, banjo, mandolin, and bagpipes, to name a few.

Musicians love working on the show. Like everything else on the show, it is a true collaboration. It's unusual for musicians to be given the freedom to improvise in this kind of job.

Let's use the example of a bassoonist. When the musician arrives at the studio, Mike and Nick will give him or her the music and set up the scene in the episode—let's say, an episode in which there is a duck. Mike and Nick will tell the musician, "Okay, you are the duck in this scene. Play this like you are a duck." Or they will bring a baritone sax player into the studio and set up a scene in which Green Puppy is angry. They will tell him or her, "Okay, you are Green Puppy, who is angry in this scene. Play this like Green Puppy."

At the end of the recording session, the musician is told one more thing: "Play the funniest, most bizarre sound you can make on your instrument." All those unusual sounds are put into the *Blue's Clues* music library for further use—sounds that are fun and entertaining for little children.

Mike and Nick work with some of the world's most talented musicians to create the music for *Blue's Clues*. Ray Charles and the Persuasions, among others, played on the video, *Blue's Big Musical*.

They have one more claim to fame. Nick is the voice of the character Mr. Salt on the show and Mike is the voice of Mailbox. Interestingly, among their friends and family, they are more famous for that than they are for their groundbreaking music!

THE *BLUE'S CLUES* LIVE SHOW

Since 1999, the *Blue's Clues* live show has wowed kids and parents alike in more than 120 cities across the country. More than 2.25 million people have attended some 1,000 performances. As *Los Angeles Times* writer Lynne Heffley said in her review of the show, "*Sesame Street* does it, *Rugrats* does it, and *Arthur* does it, but *Blue's Clues* does it better. *Blue's Clues Live!*, one of the latest TV shows–turned stage extravaganza, is a veritable goody bag of musical fun." The first traveling show was such a success that a new show, *Blue's Big Birthday Party*, hit the road in January 2002 and will run through 2003.

If you've ever been to a big-stage, live theatrical performance for kids, you probably know they can be sleepers—downright painful for adults and disappointing for children. At Nickelodeon, Nick Jr., and *Blue's Clues*, they have a name for those kinds of shows—"skip and wave"—where the characters merely dance around the stage, miming and acting Kabuki-style. There is very little real connection between the characters and the audience.

Once again, Nick Jr. and the *Blue's Clues* creators started with their preschool customers. They asked themselves, "How can we best translate all the wonderful aspects of the television show to a totally different medium—the live stage—and give preschoolers a magnificent, theatrical experience?" They knew that most producers try replicate the television show exactly, which doesn't work. They would have to do something totally different.

The producer of the live show, Jonathan Hochwald of Clear Channel Family Entertainment, had worked extensively with Nickelodeon on other shows, but never for preschoolers. Jonathon, a former Broadway producer, had been producing theatrical performances for families for a number of years. His personal mission, in fact, was to reinvent live theater for family entertainment. His group had produced a number of innovative shows, but *Blue's Clues* presented a new opportunity and a number of challenges—

challenges he met, but not without a tremendous amount of risk taking, hard work, and collaboration with the *Blue's Clues* creators.

So what was the opportunity and what were the unique challenges? Jonathan tells a wonderful story about himself, the director, the set designer, and virtually everyone involved in the stage production. There was a moment during the preproduction when each of them recalled that transforming moment in their own lives—the moment when they experienced the magic of theater— the moment in their lives when they said, "This is the business I want to be in."

Like the creators of the *Blue's Clues* music, they realized they had a unique opportunity to introduce children to their first live, theatrical experience. The cast and crew wanted it to be as magical for the kids as it had been for them. They were committed to making the show as special and memorable for kids as possible. From that moment on, that commitment drove everything they did.

The challenges, however, were huge. First, how do you produce a show where there is only one live character and every other character in the television show is animated? Second, the host of the television show could not appear in the live show because of his television shoot schedule, so they had to get another actor. What if the kids ran out of the theater crying because it wasn't the real Steve? Third, the television show works largely as a result of the interactivity between the host and cohosts—the at-home viewers. Television is very intimate and up-close. How do you get 2,000 kids to interact with one character in a huge theater when most of them have never even been in a big theater and it is their first experience of being in a room with 2,000 other kids their age?

Jonathan knew that if you want breakthrough, you sometimes have to recruit talent who have nontraditional experience. Director Gip Hoppe and set designer Dave Gallo, for example, were the best in their fields, but neither of them had experience in family entertainment. Gip is a gifted playwrite and director and owns his own theater company, and Dave has created amazing sets for

Broadway shows such as *The Lion in Winter, A View from the Bridge,* and *Thoroughly Modern Millie.* But this was a new challenge for both of them as well as the producer and television show creators.

They would have to take some huge leaps and it would take trust—trust between Nickelodeon, Nick Jr., the creators of *Blue's Clues,* and the producer and director of the live show. Everyone was working from the same vision of creating theatrical magic for preschoolers, but realizing that vision was not easy. For the live show to fully and accurately reflect the brand, the original creators had to have integral roles. Although they weren't the experts in live theater, they were experts about their customer. They knew that certain features of the television show had to be incorporated into the live show if it was to ring true and be meaningful for the kids.

It was another lesson for the creators in fighting hard for the right things and letting go so other people can do what they do best. Once the creators had established the foundation and ensured that the writing, set design, costumes, and music (magnificently composed by Mike and Nick) met the television show's standards, they let the producers go—but not until then.

Working closely with the creators of the television show, the producer and director set out to capture what makes the live theatrical experience so special—the relationship between the audience and the cast. In most theatrical shows for children, the characters' lines are prerecorded. There is a call for response from the audience, but it is forced. There is no spontaneous give and take between the audience and the cast, so the energy is lost.

Since the audience connection to the characters was key to creating the magic, Gip gave the actors plenty of room for improvisation. He knew that if he gave the actors the experience of connecting with the audience, if they could feel the power of that connection, the magic would happen naturally for the kids. You could say he empowered and challenged the actors and gave them a good time, and as a result, the parents and kids had an unforgettable experience.

Even in live theater for adults, actors rarely have that kind of freedom. They have to follow the script closely, if not exactly, so they can connect with the audience through only the author's words. Because the actors were given the freedom to improvise and respond in the moment, their relationship with the audience was real and evolved over the course of the show so that by the time the show was over, cast and audience were solidly connected. They had a relationship.

As Tom Mizer, who played Steve in the first show, said, "It was one of the most incredible experiences of my life. Because I and the other cast members were allowed to improvise, there was this amazing flow of energy back and forth between us and the kids. The kids gave us so much. They brought us into their world and taught us how to play, which is probably why about 75 percent of the original cast and crew came back after the first season—something that rarely happens in live theatrical shows, because the schedule is so grueling."

Tom also commented, "I now know what it is like to be an Elvis or Billy Joel. From the moment I walked on the stage, kids all the way in the back row of a 2,000 seat theater were standing in their seats, stomping their feet, calling my name." Tom was careful to note that he wasn't the real star—he was only acting. The real star is the television host.

The overall show itself also evolved over time. As the actors improvised and ad-libbed, funny things would happen, lucky flukes. The actors learned what particularly pleased the audience and what didn't, so that the show at the end of the run was very different from the show at the beginning of the run. It was always a work in progress. As with the television show, they listened to the audience and followed its lead.

In addition to entertaining the kids, Gip created comedic moments on a number of different levels so that parents would enjoy the show. And he succeeded. Of the thousands of letters received by Nickelodeon, Nick Jr., and *Blue's Clues* about the show, there was not one complaint in any of them about the show. It was a miracle. It was the first time any of the members of the cast and crew had been a part of a show in which there was not a single complaint from anyone.

Jonathan confesses, however, to waking up in the middle of the night in a cold sweat before the first show. Would the kids interact and would they embrace the Tom in the role of Steve? If that didn't happen, the show would fail and so would he.

But from the moment the kids and parents entered the theater, they were mesmerized. Each child received a Handy Dandy Notebook like the one the host in the television show uses in every episode; it's also used by the kids at home as they watch the show, so it is a very popular item. As they are escorted to their seats and before the show begins, they are met by the first character, Curt, which is short for curtain—an element of the show that takes over the theater. The curtain, which is actually a giant puppet who can talk and see, gets the kids to interact from the moment they step into the theater. Curt welcomes everyone and gets them excited about what's going to happen.

The curtain opens to a bare stage with a single television set. The theatrical Steve is trapped inside the set. Using a skidoo moment in which the host and characters are magically transported to another place, just as they do in the television show—the kids are able to get him out of the set and onto the stage. Then the big moment happens. The curtain goes up again and there is a full-scale set of the outside of Steve's house on the show. At this point, Steve talks to the kids about the magic of the theater. He explains to them that in the theater, if you use your imagination things become real.

From there Steve proceeds to give them a short education on the theater, pointing out things like the lights, the ushers, the sound, and so on. He has made the sale. He is not the real Steve, but they have embraced him just the same. The magic has begun.

From the moment the show starts, kids are screaming, talking back to Steve, and waving their Handy Dandy Notebooks. The magic builds throughout the show to the grand finale, which is a big party—and what a party it is. By now, the kids are dancing in their seats and in the aisles. Some are storming the stage to touch Steve, just like in a rock concert. One little girl was so moved by the whole experience that she took off all her clothes and ran to the front of the stage to see Steve, with mother chasing behind her. They had done it! They had given preschoolers a magical theatrical experience, which kids and parents would never forget.

INTERNATIONAL VERSION OF *BLUE'S CLUES*

Diversity is a hot topic in most companies today. It's a mandatory training program for managers in just about every company, but how many companies truly live it? The earlier people learn to accept and appreciate differences, the better. If kids can learn to appreciate differences at the age of three or four, they won't have to go to classes when they are adults.

Diversity has always been one of the guiding principles of *Blue's Clues,* which is one of the reasons it is not just a U.S. phenomenon—it's an international phenomenon as well. Mr. Salt is white and Mrs. Pepper is black, and both have French accents. Blue, the costar, is a girl puppy instead of a boy. The music comes from virtually every corner of the globe.

One of the show's most successful episodes was one that focused on deafness. With the help of deaf actress Marlee Matlin, Steve taught preschoolers sign language. Ever since then, sign language is incorporated into every episode. The response from the deaf community has been overwhelming. *Blue's Clues* even won a GLAD Award for promoting deaf awareness in the media.

When *Blue's Clues* went international, it was a natural because of its emphasis on diversity, but it was still an American show. Many countries around the world are resistant to American shows that are dubbed, particularly children's shows, because they fail to

The following message appeared on the Nick Jr.
Web site message board for parents:

Blue Is Great with Bilingual Kids!

My son Daniel has always loved *Blue's Clues*,
since he was about eight months old. We would
sit down and watch the show every day without
fail until he was almost two years old. Then we
went to stay with his grandparents in Mexico
for one year. For the first week he whined a
lot, wanting to see his *Blue's Clues*. Then I
discovered that one of his cousins watched the
show in Spanish every morning. My son was so
happy to see the show again. He learned how to
sing the Mail Song in English and Spanish,
along with all of the other songs. Kudos to
Blue for capturing the attention of every young
child, no matter what language they speak!

teach children about their own culture. In the United Kingdom, for example, guidelines restrict the amount of foreign preschool programming allowed on the air.

The *Blue's Clues* creators considered their potential international customer from the start, designing the show so that it could be easily customized to a particular country. *Blue's Clues* provides the raw material for the show so it can be produced with a local host, with whom the children would better identify. The story line, animated characters, and actions are the same; the cultural context and host are different.

Very few foreign television shows for preschoolers are produced in this way. Most of them are dubbed and shown "as is," with the host from the originating country. *Blue's Clues* creators hope to set a trend that allows more countries to air top-notch, high-quality programming for preschoolers that is adapted to their own culture.

In the U.K., where the show is anglicized, it is a runaway hit. The show's host is Kevin; the character Mailbox is Post Box; and the characters Shovel and Pail are Bucket and Spade. In the four years since it has been on the air, it has become one of the most-watched preschool programs on television. *Blue's Clues* consumer products have been flying off the shelves since their introduction in 2001. The first week a video of an episode was introduced, it became the best-selling video in all of England—and that includes videos for adults as well.

Blue's Clues also has become a part of pop culture in Korea, where it airs in prime time on KBS TV network, the equivalent of the BBC in the U.K. It outperforms the top two preschool television shows, including the show that is the equivalent of *Sesame Street*.

The show's host is Mr. Shim, whose popularity in Korea is similar to that of Oprah Winfrey's in the U.S. His fame, which preceded his taking on the role of *Blue's Clues* host, has helped to make the show wildly popular there.

Customizing the show does require a number of changes. For example, the *Blue's Clues* creators in the U.S., have to be careful

to never show a fork in an episode—there are no forks in Korea, only spoons. In an episode where Steve has a dream that he is Elvis, Mr. Shim instead dressed as a traditional Korean dancer with a tasseled hat.

Blue's Clues also airs in dozens of other countries around the world—some 60 countries in all. With the exception of the U.K. and Korea, the episodes are either dubbed or shown in English. *Blue's Clues* is working hard to convince more countries to adapt and localize the show as they do in Korea and the U.K.

CONSUMER PRODUCTS AND LICENSING

One of the best examples of how *Blue's Clues* stays focused on their customer is the way in which they go about creating and producing the vast array of consumer products, which include everything from books to CD-ROMs, videos, educational toys, clothes, and food products. It is a story unto its own, which will be told in Chapter 6, "Clue In to Your Brand."

CLUES FOR Staying Focused on Your Customer

People cannot be pushed, prodded, or bribed into staying focused on the customer and providing superior service: They have to be inspired to do so. When people truly care about the customer and believe in their company's product or service, phenomenal things can happen—there is an enormous release of energy. Here are some things you can do to keep your company, department, or team focused on the customer:

- Keep the mission statement in front of people at all times.

- Constantly bring the mission alive for people—make the connections between their tasks and the mission.

- Communicate and teach the importance of staying focused on the customer every chance possible—make it a way of life, not a program.

- Never assume you know what your customer wants, needs, and thinks.

- Stay in constant communication with the customer—keep probing and listening.

- Learn from your competition and improve upon the best of what they do.

- Get everyone thinking and talking "breakthrough"—take risks and go against conventional thinking.

- Keep people emotionally connected to the customer.

- Encourage people to ask "Why not?"

- Tell lots of customer stories—stories about how the company has helped or pleased customers. Circulate positive customer letters.

SUGGESTED EXERCISE

Make flip charts of the bulleted items outlined in the previous section. Break the members of your team into groups of three or four. Ask each group to rate the entire team on each item on a scale of 1 to 100 percent. If a group thinks the team does a really good job of staying focused on the mission, for example, they would rate the team between 85 percent and 100 percent. If a group rates the team below 85 percent but above 70 percent, the team does a fair job of staying focused on the mission. Anything less than 70 percent means the group thinks the team needs dramatic improvement on that item. Each group must be prepared to defend its ranking for each item.

After each group is done writing down the various ratings on the flip chart (provide one for each group), ask each group to share its ratings and the reasons for the ratings with the entire team. This will generate a lively discussion among the team and provide a starting point for making improvements. Following this exercise, you can have the team plan for staying more customer-focused. (This applies to internal customers as well as external customers.)

CLUES FOR Furthering Your Career by Serving Others

Albert Schweitzer once said: "I don't know what your destiny will be, but one thing I know: the only ones among you who will be really happy are those who will have sought and found how to serve." If you look at your work as an opportunity to serve others—whether external customers or coworkers—it can improve the way you think and feel about your job. When your job has meaning, you naturally perform better.

Having a customer focus also impacts your success. People are more inclined to help and support those who help them. Your relationships with others are a major factor in your career success. If you have contact with external customers and serve them well, others within the company take note of it.

Here are some suggestions that can help you serve your customers better:

- Identify who your primary and secondary customers are at work. Determine who needs your support in order to accomplish their objectives.

- Talk to your customers and ask them for feedback on how you can serve them better.

- Instead of focusing solely on your own work needs, try to anticipate the needs of your customers.

■ Pay attention. Try to understand your customers and look for ways to be helpful to them.

CHAPTER Summary

In order for a company to fulfill its mission, everyone within the organization must make the customer the focus of everything they do. They must respect the customer, listen to the customer, and never assume that they know what the customer thinks or how he or she will respond. The clearer the company is about their customer, the greater the likelihood they will be able to meet customer expectations. The company must continuously strive to understand the customer and the customer's changing needs by probing, listening, and staying in constant communication with them.

The customer should always be the focus of any decisions made about the product. If the people of the organization keep searching for the customer's unmet needs and if they keep trying to serve them in unique and innovative ways, the company will be better able to distinguish itself from the competition. The more the company goes against conventional thinking and thinks "breakthrough," the more the customer will see the company or product as being in a class of its own.

Clue # 2

When you know your *customer*, love your customer, and keep him or her the *focus* of everything you do, you won't have to worry about the competition. You will be in a class of your own.

CHAPTER 3

Clue In to Your Research

RESEARCH REDEFINED

In Chapter 1, we said that the *Blue's Clues* mission—to empower, challenge, and build the self-esteem of preschoolers while making them laugh—is the guiding light, the foundation, the conscience for everything they do. The *Blue's Clues* creators are determined in the way they ensure that every single aspect of their business— from the television show to the live show, books, and consumer products—is true to the mission. They fight for the mission and their customer with great conviction and confidence.

What makes them so confident? Some of it has to do with the creators' personalities and competencies, but mostly it has to do with research. Like the parent company, Nickelodeon, they are research fanatics. They are a true fact-based company. You could say that research is one of the primary protectors of the mission. It's also the basis for justifying and explaining everything they do. In effect, it's a sales tool.

At *Blue's Clues,* they not only do a tremendous amount of research, but the research department is an integral part of the decision-making process. Research does more than deliver information. They work empathetically and collaboratively with the creative people. They provide guidance that enriches the creative product.

In most companies, research takes a back seat and is sometimes looked upon with skepticism and disdain. It is a powerful tool, yet an undervalued and underutilized one. At *Blue's Clues*, research is defined as follows: Research is the ongoing process that guides and supports every aspect of the business in fulfilling the mission.

WHOLE-BRAIN THINKERS

Have you ever been in a room with a bunch of researchers or financial types on one side and creative types on the other? It can be deadly. It's as though they are from different planets. They don't speak the same language. They operate from two different sides of the brain.

The *Blue's Clues* creators, on the other hand, are whole-brain thinkers, one of the reasons the show is so successful. They are highly creative in their thinking and take brainstorming to a whole new level; at the same time, they are scientific and disciplined in their approach to everything. Each set of skills works to facilitate the other. Because they are disciplined, their brainstorming results in great creative content, which enables the show to fulfill its mission. The mission is the guide, but the rigorous discipline of research provides the information, which keeps everyone honest and on the right path. Nothing much happens without input from research.

FROM THE BEGINNING

Many companies skimp on research in the developmental phase of a product or service because they don't want to spend the money. The product fails or falls short of expectations set for it because the company didn't do its homework. And then production or marketing or some other department gets blamed for its failure when the real problem was in the product design.

A great deal of research went into the *Blue's Clues* mission and show, which is one reason the show was destined for success. As we mentioned earlier, one of the creators, Angela Santomero, came out of Nickelodeon's research department. She and the other creators are visionaries whose intuition—the place where all great creative innovation comes from—was informed by a tremendous amount of research. By the time the pilot was created, they knew they had a hit because the research told them so. They had done extensive research about how preschoolers learn, how they develop, and how they watch television. They also tested the pilot in its earliest stages of production with preschoolers themselves. In fact, at *Blue's Clues,* they call research their "secret sauce." They know they've got it right before they show it to anyone else, because they've proven it to themselves through research.

The prominent role research would play in the show's future success was solidified when Alice Wilder, a classmate of Angela's at Teachers's College in New York, joined the team just after the production of the pilot. Alice was working on her dissertation on the effectiveness of instructional programs for students with learning disabilities when Angela showed her the pilot and asked for her feedback. As Alice described it, "I literally cried when I saw it. The show applied virtually everything I had known about children and had learned about child development. To see my learnings put into action in such a powerful, creative fashion—in a way that I knew would have a huge impact on preschoolers everywhere— was one of the most moving experiences of my life."

Angela had another reason for showing the video to Alice. She hoped that Alice would be intrigued enough to join the *Blue's Clues* team and head up the research department while finishing her dissertation. The original creators envisioned a research department that would embrace the *Blue's Clues* mission—that could see what they saw in terms of the show's potential. Even more important, they knew they needed someone who had knowledge of child development and a vision for what research could be in the life of the show. They needed someone who would be an integral part of the creative process and the decision-making process—someone who could collaborate and embrace the creative process, but also give validation and credence to what they knew in their guts and challenge them when they were off base.

When something is destined to be, the decision making becomes easy. It feels so right that circumstance or reason have little or no impact on the final decision. Alice was on a path to finish her doctoral studies when the opportunity presented itself. She couldn't say no; she would do both. After all, *Blue's Clues* was the perfect laboratory for applying in the real world everything she knew in academia. Like the original creators of the show, Alice would prove to be a pioneer, too. By reinventing the role of research, she played a major role in reinventing children's television.

THE PERSONAL STORY

*W**hen I was a kid I was never a very good student, because I didn't have much motivation to learn. I could never see the meaning or relevance of what was being taught in school to my own life. My response to most of what I was supposed to learn was, "So what?"*

I am a living example of the powerful influence a teacher and mentor can have in a student's life, at any age. I was a freshman in college when the instructor of the psychology course I was taking, Mary Ann Foley, sparked the fires of my intellect and opened a whole new world of learning for me. She saw something in me and tended the fire. What she taught me was so fascinating, so relevant, and meaningful to me that it set me on a path of lifelong learning about psychology, child development, and research—the field in which I eventually earned a doctorate.

Life sometimes comes together through an unusual sequence of events, which in retrospect seems perfectly timed and planned. Around the time of my in-tellectual awakening I saw the movie, Big, *starring Tom Hanks, whose character is a child in the body of an adult. He is an adult with a child's mind and is in charge of toy development at a toy company. He is highly successful in his posi-tion because he feels and thinks like a child.*

When I saw that movie I thought to myself, "That's it. I want to be like Tom Hanks—I want to be the voice of the child in an adult world. I want to use the knowledge I have of children and development to give them experiences that are meaningful and relevant to their lives. That's why working at Blue's Clues *is a dream come true for me—I get to be the preschool voice for whom the show is made.*

Alice Wilder, Ed. D.
Director of Research and Development

GAINING RESPECT FOR RESEARCH

Research can be a powerful tool, but only if the people who impact the design, production, and delivery of the product or service realize how it can enhance their own effectiveness. If you think of research as the tool that keeps you connected to your customers—by telling you who they are, what they want, how they think, and what they think about your product—everyone in the organization should be sitting at the feet of research, hungering for what research has to share with them.

If research is to have that kind of credibility and value for the people of the organization, you have to change the commonly held attitudes, beliefs, and assumptions that people have about research. By the same token, researchers have to change the way they work. They can't just say yes or no; they have to work with the creative process. They have to apply their research properly and creatively if it is to be effective.

Because Angela knew how valuable research would be to the success of *Blue's Clues,* she made sure there was money for it in the production budget. She wanted a dedicated research department for formative, day-to-day research. Research would be used in more than an advisory capacity; it would be part of the creative team. They still had the challenge of getting everyone within the production company to understand the importance of research. Researchers also had to learn how to give input in a way that respected the vision of the creative people working on the product. How they made that happen is just one more example of how savvy *Blue's Clues* is about people and the creative process.

In the beginning, Angela and Alice helped every department—animation, art, design, production, and so on—understand why research was so important. Because *Blue's Clues* was a curriculum-based show that had two overarching goals as its foundation—maintaining audience attention and ensuring comprehension—everyone needed to understand what made preschoolers pay attention as well as the developmental principles that impact how children learn and comprehend.

The concept was sound and made sense, but telling creative people they can't do something because research doesn't approve, usually makes them feel stifled and inhibited. The *Blue's Clues* artists, animators, and other members of the team had to become believers through experience. Research could not be forced. Initially, there was a tremendous amount of resistance to the idea of research playing such a prominent role in the production. It took a long, hard struggle to get to the point today where research is completely integrated into the entire process.

In the beginning, Alice shadowed Angela as she met with people throughout the production company and the ancillary businesses. With the eye of a scientist and a keen sense of what works with preschoolers and what doesn't, she would quietly inform

Angela why something would or wouldn't work. Angela often had a gut sense that was right in sync with Alice, but Alice had a depth of knowledge and could explain why Angela's gut was on target. Angela, who already had credibility with the people involved in the production, would voice Alice's concerns. Ever so slowly, she and Alice brought research to the forefront of the process.

Before long, the creative synergy between research and production began to build. They realized that Alice had knowledge that was so fundamental and essential to what they were trying to achieve with their piece of the end product that they started seeking her out. In one instance, Alice explained why a particular scene planned for an episode wouldn't work. When the animator heard Alice's feedback and explanation, she was relieved—she had been struggling with the scene and knew it wasn't right, but didn't know why.

One by one, people and departments became believers in research and they had a foundation of trust from which to work, a foundation that was essential to the accomplishment of the mission. It wasn't just what Alice said that made them listen but how she said it. She is never academic in her explanation and she never tells creative staff they can't do something. She explains why it will or will not work and then brainstorms with the person options that will work.

One of the reasons researchers often are not better received is because they don't know how to talk to the people they are trying to influence. As Alice puts it, "I draw on three things in order to achieve understanding with creative people: scientific knowledge, common sense, and my perspective, which is that of a three- to four-year-old." You could say she is a whole-brain researcher. She tests it against her gut: How does the three- to four-year-old in her respond? She tests it against her scientific knowledge, which, by the way, she always keeps to herself. She communicates what is in her gut and in her head in a way that makes common sense to the creative person. Alice is careful to note, however, that research would not have the influence it has today if Angela had not put so much importance on it and if Alice had not worked in a collaborative fashion, influencing instead of dictating.

USING RESEARCH TO DEFINE
THE CORE PRODUCT

Many companies write lofty mission statements, but they fail to fulfill them because they have no overarching philosophy. They define the "what," meaning what we are going to do, but they fail to properly address the "how," how we are going to fulfill the mission. The how is what sets you apart from the competition. It defines the key attribute or attributes of the product or service. One of the reasons *Blue's Clues* is a phenomenon is because they spent an enormous amount of time up front defining the philosophy and the "how."

Here's how they used research to define their product and execute the mission. At *Blue's Clues,* they knew they wanted to challenge, empower, and build the self-esteem of preschoolers while making them laugh—that was their mission. It was no small challenge. They decided to do it by developing a "thinking skills" program, which would provide preschoolers with kindergarten readiness skills. The how is what set them apart—it was different from what anyone else was doing—the how was what enabled them to push children's television to a new level.

From the beginning, the creators determined that they wanted to stretch the mind of preschoolers. To do that, they had to understand what preschoolers know and then challenge them to know more. They wanted to facilitate the invisible process of development.

They established from the beginning that the show would be based on three types of knowledge or research:

1. The preschoolers' level of development

2. The formal features of television and how they can facilitate learning for preschoolers

3. The educational curriculum preschoolers needed to prepare them for kindergarten

They continuously asked how and resisted the temptation to make it up. Instead, they relied on their research, which told them they could stretch the minds of preschoolers by doing the following:

- Providing challenging and fun activities and games throughout the show

- Teaching them thinking skills in the context of their own everyday life experiences

- Providing a model for parents and caregivers of how to appropriately interact and challenge preschoolers when they are not watching the show

- Presenting problem-solving situations that are common to preschoolers' everyday life

- Providing a model of multiculturalism by exposing them to racial and ethnic diversity

At the core of the show is the educational curriculum, which defines precisely what they want their customers to be able to do as a result of watching the show. If every company was as clear about what they want their product to do for their customer and stayed true to that, there would be a lot more successful companies.

Earlier, we talked about the importance of companies having a clear philosophy. One of the *Blue's Clues* philosophies is that preschoolers learn through everything they do and therefore learning should be a part of everyday life. That's why the show is story-driven rather than curriculum-driven. The curriculum is intended to be invisible, which is why many parents don't fully realize the educational value of the show. Most adults don't associate entertainment and fun with learning because of their own early learning experiences; that is precisely what makes *Blue's Clues* a phenomenon.

Throughout each episode are a series of games, each of which is designed to teach a specific thinking skill—games that are played in the context of the show's story line. In a game designed to give preschoolers matching skills, for example, by showing them a bunch of baby chicks with different hats—two of which have the same hat—they don't just ask the kids to match the hats. They set up a story that the chicks need to find their friends who have matching hats so they can go for a snack together. Snack time is a big event for preschoolers, so this particular episode teaches the matching skill in the context of something they do every day.

Who knows where some of us might be if learning had been presented to us in such a relevant, entertaining way when we were growing up? If *life* and *learning* had been synonymous, some of us wouldn't have stopped the learning process when we left school.

The *Blue's Clues* creators believe in the philosophy and the show so strongly that they often talk about *Blue's Clues* helping to ensure a kid's place in Harvard. You may laugh at that statement, but it's not that far-fetched if you consider how impressionable two- to five-year-olds are and how formative those years are; and you consider the sophistication of the *Blue's Clues* curriculum and the fact that the show really does teach kids how to think and solve problems.

As a manager, how many times have you bemoaned the fact that people just don't know how to think? Or maybe you have struggled with employees or even other managers to whom you could teach something in one situation, but if presented with a situation that was slightly different at another time, they wouldn't be able to perform. They couldn't transfer learning from one situation to another. They can learn by rote memorization, but they have difficulty analyzing and solving problems, probably because they were programmed to learn by repetition and memorization in school.

At *Blue's Clues,* they use the term *far transfer,* the preschooler's ability to apply a thinking skill learned early in the episode in other contexts, particularly in the context of their own lives. For example, let's say an episode is designed to teach shapes. In the context of a game, they will show objects that are in the shape of a square or a circle or a rectangle.

Let's say the rectangle object is a graham cracker. If the preschooler only associates *rectangle* with *graham cracker,* there has been no transfer of learning. If, on the other hand, the preschooler is sitting at the breakfast table the next day and points to the light switch and says, "rectangle," real learning has taken place—there has been a far transfer.

The philosophy that learning should take place in the context of a preschooler's everyday life has an enormous impact on the *Blue's Clues* curriculum. It allows them to teach just about anything. Episodes have covered topics such as math, science, physics, geography, planets and outer space, time and space, and environments, to name a few. The thinking is that you can teach kids anything if it is relevant to their world.

When you teach children geography, for example, you teach them that there is a world beyond their own homes. To preschoolers, that world starts at their homes and expands into the neighborhoods, so you can teach them about what is in their neighborhood. So you introduce the concept of geography in a very elementary way—in a way they can relate to.

If you are teaching them about time, you don't teach them all of the mechanics of telling time because developmentally it is an abstract concept, but by teaching it visually and concretely you can teach them the concept of time. In the episode on time, for example, they presented time in the context of waiting, because that's a lot of what a preschooler does—wait. The show's host, Steve, asks the animated character Mailbox when the mail will arrive and Mailbox says, "In a minute," a phrase preschoolers probably hear often. Steve points to a watch on the screen and tells the kids that when the big hand goes all the way around to the 12, it will be one minute. He actually sits and waits for one whole minute while the hand goes around.

The foundation has been set for teaching them the more abstract concepts of how to tell time at a later date when they are ready. They are able to teach things that preschoolers wouldn't learn otherwise at this age, because they make things visual and concrete.

The *Blue's Clues* curriculum provides a solid foundation for future learning. The curriculum includes a whole range of thinking skills as well as language, perceptual, and social skills. Here are some examples of the thinking skills the show teaches:

Sorting. Preschoolers are able to group items by the way they look or the various ways they are used. A spoon, plate, and cup are all objects we use to eat. Shoes, socks, pants, and shirts are all items that one wears.

Categorizing and classifying. Preschoolers are able to systematically arrange and identify objects that belong in the same or different classes or categories. In a *Blue's Clues* scene, children might be asked to put a red object away with other red objects. Or they may be asked which object does not belong with a group of objects that are living.

Differentiating and discriminating. Preschoolers can make distinctions among disparate or distinguishing characteristics. In a series of pictures they might be asked which objects are bigger or which objects are round.

Predicting and anticipating. Preschoolers are able to declare in advance what they think will happen or will come next. They may be asked questions such as "Which way will the object move from here?" or "What comes next?"

What happened and why. Preschoolers are able to explore information that is presented to them by understanding the events that took place and questioning all of its component parts. Kids might be shown a frustrating situation, a shirt with paint on it, or a person running but falling and asked to explore how they got that way.

Ordering and sequencing. Preschoolers are able to order a set of elements that together form a coherent relationship. They might be asked, "Do you brush your teeth and then put the toothpaste on the toothbrush and then rinse?"

Patterning. Preschoolers are able to fill in or complete a reliable sample of traits, acts, tendencies, or other observable characteristics. They might be asked to determine what article of clothing comes next in the closet by size and category or which color and shape sprinkle comes next on the cake.

Matching. Preschoolers are able to note the features of an object that identify it and use that information to equate objects. For example, they might be asked to match an object or person to the painting they fell out of, hats on chicks, or a shadow with the object that made it.

Inferential problem-solving skills. Preschoolers are able to arrive at a definitive solution based on reasoning from evidence or examples. In each episode they are given three sets of clues in order to solve the puzzle of the day. They might be given the bricks, wolf, and pigs clue set to solve the mystery, "The Three Little Pigs."

Associating. Preschoolers are able to join objects by essential similarities. For example, they might show three objects—a ball, a moon, and a snowball.

Analogies. Preschoolers are able to identify a resemblance among objects that are otherwise unlike. Smile is to _____ as frown is to _____; Elephant is to _____ as mouse is to _____. (Do you remember seeing some of these questions on tests you have taken as an adult?)

Relational concepts. Preschoolers are able to associate and differentiate properties that hold between an ordered pair of objects. For example, top–bottom, first–last, right–left.

The curriculum also focuses on language skills. Preschoolers acquire vocabulary at an incredibly rapid rate. The ability to use language, verbal and physical, holds the key to acquiring and expressing knowledge. Through the show, preschoolers are able to do the following:

- Acquire word meanings in the context of the day's adventure

- Label and question

- Interact and talk through the learning process so that they own the content for themselves

The show is also quite sophisticated in how it teaches perceptual skills, which involves the mental grasp of objects and concepts through the senses. For the visual, for example, kids might be asked to "Look at this mess of toys." The lights are turned out and one is put away. When the lights come on, the child is asked, "Which toy did we put away?" To develop the auditory sense, they might invite kids to speak softly and loudly so they can discriminate between sounds.

The curriculum also addresses social and emotional issues. One of the overall goals of the show is to build the self-esteem of pre-schoolers. Self-esteem is built in children when they feel success-ful, feel their peers believe they are successful, and adults think they are successful. Every episode of *Blue's Clues* concentrates on modeling appropriate interaction among the characters, empha-sizing attributes such as helpfulness, manners, cooperation, respect, sharing, turn taking, compassion, tolerance, and cooperation.

The curriculum encourages their emotional development by addressing life skills, social problem solving, and a whole range of emotions and issues concerning feelings—issues such as conflict resolution, sibling rivalry, and facial expressions. Each episode chal-lenges preschoolers to understand and identify feelings through games and characters—feelings such as happy, sad, proud, grate-ful, brave, jealous, scared, tired, angry, shy, anxious, and nervous.

In one episode, for example, entitled "Blue's Sad Day," the main character, Blue, who you will recall is a preschooler who looks like a puppy, is sad because Green Puppy keeps knocking down Blue's block tower. The creators wanted to teach kids a dif-ferent way to deal with situations that are all too familiar to them. In the episode, Blue gives Green Puppy a few of her blocks. Blue understands that Green Puppy isn't trying to be mean—he just likes to knock things down. When he gets some of his own blocks, he no longer needs to knock down Blue's block tower.

As you can see, many of the messages on the show apply to older children and adults as well, which is probably why the show has such wide appeal. It reminds one of Robert Fulghum's book, *All I Really Need to Know I Learned in Kindergarten*. Everything we need to know, we can learn from *Blue's Clues*—particularly in terms of how to relate and interact with one another.

How they teach these skills is scientific and creative at the same time. As we mentioned in Chapter 2, one of the ways they rein-force learning and extend it beyond the show is by using mantras

Dear *Blue's Clues,*

I just wanted to thank the *Blue's Clues* producers and creative staff for coming up with some of the greatest ideas for your shows. The one about changing dreams was fabulous. My three-year-old was having nightmares, so we sat down with the family and watched the episode on dreams together. Then we drew dream catchers and the ladybugs she was having nightmares about and changed them into balloons—just like the girl in the show changed her monster into a cake!

I also appreciated the episodes on dealing with feelings, finding things, and most of all the one about what to do when you are frustrated. My daughter will stop now after just one viewing and sing the line from the show—stop, breathe, and think.

So once again, thank you very much for your creativeness. Your efforts and talents are noticed and appreciated by us parents. Your ideas help make our jobs easier.

Thanks,

Stacey Taylor

and songs that are repeated over and over. At the end of each episode, just before they solve the puzzle, they chant, "Think! Think! Think!" That's probably a good mantra for all of us, particularly people working in companies and organizations. Another mantra is "go back, go back, go back," to be used when they lose something.

The intent is that parents and caregivers will use these mantras and songs with kids at times other than when they are watching the show. Sometimes kids use them to help their parents. One of the most clever mantras is the one they encourage preschoolers to use when they are frustrated: "Stop, think, and breathe!" One mother wrote to relay a story about how her three-year-old had helped her by reminding her to "stop, think, and breathe" on a day when she was having a particularly stressful time.

The curriculum with which we just acquainted you is the primary tool used by the research department to ensure that each episode meets the goals of the show and fulfills the mission. The research department not only develops the curriculum based on a tremendous amount of research, but also uses it to educate, guide, and direct the various departments who produce the episodes.

Earlier we talked about the concept of far transfer. How does this explanation of the *Blue's Clues* curriculum transfer to other businesses and companies? It shows the lengths to which a company must go if it is to provide a breakthrough product or service that meets customer needs on a consistent basis. It also demonstrates the amount of research required to ensure that the how—how a company tries to fulfill the mission—actually hits the mark.

SAVING TIME AND MONEY THROUGH RESEARCH

In some companies, research provides a wealth of information at the beginning of the product or service development phase and then disappears from the scene. But not involving this group every step of the way can cost a company a tremendous amount of time and money. Each episode is researched three times during production, more preproduction research than any other children's television show, and it pays off.

Blue's Clues invests time and money up front in order to save money in the long run. Each episode takes approximately one year to produce. A writer thinks of an idea for an episode, starting either with the story line or with the skill to be taught. The writer discusses the idea with research. If the idea works creatively for the writer and the preschool audience, he or she works with research to develop a goal sheet, which identifies what the writer wishes to accomplish in the episode. The goals, of course, are based on the curriculum and the needs of the audience. When the script is in the development phase, it is rigorously examined and questioned.

Once the script draft is developed and approved, it is tested in three different schools in the New York tristate area. A variety of schools participate in the testing—public schools, private schools, day care centers, pre-K schools, and Head Start programs—to ensure that they are reaching an audience that is reflective of the television show audience.

Each of the three testings is conducted by three researchers. The writer attends, simply to observe. A total of 30 kids, ranging from two to five years of age, divided into three separate groups, participate in the testing. At this point, the show is in the form of a storybook—pictures on paper, narrated by one of the three people doing the research. In this first round, researchers make detailed notes that reflect whether the episode is getting the responses it was intended to get at various points in the episode. Are the kids able to follow the story? Are they paying attention? What are they saying in response to our questions? How do their responses vary by age? Is learning taking place?

Each episode of *Blue's Clues* is researched three times during production, more preproduction research than any other children's television show.

After the first testing, the data is compiled and the findings are written up and presented to everyone involved in producing the episode—the show's creators, producers, episode associate producer, writer, episode director, animation, design, and art. Here's where research is so critical in keeping the team motivated and focused on the goals. By hearing directly from the kids through the research process, the people who are producing the product get direct and objective feedback, feedback that informs and inspires them. Research, of course, is there to explain why kids did or did not respond in a certain way and to engage the team in creative problem solving. Changes are made in the script, not just based on the kids' responses, but also on the goals of the overall show and each episode, and an understanding of preschoolers' cognitive and social development, and how they watch television and learn.

If the changes in the script are significant, research will go back and test it in the same way. Otherwise, it is tested in rough video form—the host has been shot on the blue screen, but the animation has not been added. At this point, plans for editing, voice-overs, music, design art, and animation can all be changed, but not the live-action performance or dialogue. The results are once again noted in detail, interpreted, and presented to the team. Changes are made, and it moves to the final stage of testing.

In the final stage of testing, the episode is complete with animation, music, and so on. If the research process has worked, the episode should do what the creators intended it to do—the kids in the test should respond in the way they had hoped they would. If some things could still be improved, changes can be incorporated into other episodes in production and in all future productions.

The research process used by *Blue's Clues* in the production process provides an effective customer feedback loop. By constantly feeding information to the production team about how the customer is responding to their work, they are able to continuously raise the quality of their work and improve upon the way they meet customer needs.

USING RESEARCH TO EVALUATE IMPACT

The *Blue's Clues* people always want to know, "How are we doing?" Not just on an episode-by-episode basis, but overall, how well are they empowering, challenging, and building the self-esteem of preschoolers while making them laugh? Their "inquiring minds want to know," because it empowers them to do better. It also helps the *Blue's Clues* leaders give the people who produce the episodes a feeling of satisfaction and fulfillment in their jobs.

The primary goal of the research designed to assess the show's impact on kids evaluates how well the kids learned the thinking and prosocial skills the show has tried to teach them rather than just memorizing the correct answers. If they learn the concepts they are being taught, they will be able to apply (transfer) the knowledge and behaviors to other situations. The impact research, of course, is never conducted by the *Blue's Clues* research department, because they would be biased. It is conducted instead by independent educational institutions.

BLUE'S CLUES VIEWERS PERFORM BETTER ON STANDARDIZED TESTS

One of the most comprehensive studies was a national study conducted by Dr. Jennings Bryant, director of the University of Alabama's Institute for Communication Research. His study tracked changes that occurred over a two-year period in the cognitive abilities of preschoolers who watched the show and those with no access to the show. The primary goal of the research was to evaluate how well *Blue's Clues* met its curriculum goals. They pretested the kids in the study before any of them watched the program to see where they were developmentally. The research showed that viewers of *Blue's Clues* performed significantly better than nonviewers on a variety of measures, including standardized tests. It showed that viewers are learning—not only the content presented in the shows but they are applying outside of the show what they learn.

Dr. Bryant did another study in which he did a systematic content analysis of every single episode for two years. He tested every scene in every episode to see if it met stated goals. The study found that there were on average 7.31 educational incidents per minute in every episode. It showed that over time, *Blue's Clues* viewers demonstrated greater mastery than nonviewers on concepts such as matching, sequencing, relational concepts, and numerous other skills presented in the series. After just one month, viewers performed significantly better than nonviewers on standardized measures of important cognitive skills and abilities. The differences remained constant, and even increased in some instances, over a nine-month period.

Here is Dr. Bryant's unedited summary of conclusions from the first study:

The results of the longitudinal investigation of the effects of *Blue's Clues* in accomplishing its curriculum goals are extremely clear: Regular viewing of this breakthrough Nick Jr. program contributed substantially to preschoolers' problem-solving abilities and flexible thinking skills. Gains shown during the first season were accentuated during the second season.

Looking at the findings on information acquisition, it is obvious that viewers understood and learned the vast majority of the lessons presented in the engaging programming that conveyed the curriculum. The findings from the standardized inventories (K-ABC and K-BIT) provide compelling evidence that these lessons were internalized to such a degree that watching *Blue's Clues* regularly over the course of a year fundamentally altered the level of the children's basic problem-solving abilities.

Such evidence is exceedingly rare in the annals of children's television viewing. But it strongly supports the claim that a thoughtful curriculum conveyed in an engaging program can make a positive difference in the lives of children. In many ways, these findings return us to the promises made in the early days of television—promises that so often seemed to fall by the wayside: Television can make a positive difference in the lives of children! However, the defining conditions must be that this television features a novel, appropriate, developmentally correct curriculum and be presented in the form of enticing programming that attracts, entertains, and engages the young viewer as it unobtrusively teaches its lessons.

The *Blue's Clues* people use their impact studies to consistently improve upon their curriculum and to motivate and inspire their staff. With this kind of report card, how could they not feel an enormous sense of pride and satisfaction?

USING RESEARCH TO EXTEND THE MISSION TO OTHER PRODUCTS

Chapter 6 will discuss in more depth the *Blue's Clues* brand and all of its ancillary businesses—books, CD-ROMs, games, online content, toys, videos, clothing, etc. We can't talk about research, however, without mentioning the critical role it plays in the success of all the other businesses.

Alice Wilder's role and the process she uses in guiding the ancillary businesses are very similar to what they are for the show. Her job is to maintain the integrity of the product so that it properly reflects the brand and works to fulfill the mission of the show.

Her involvement in the ancillary businesses was a natural from the beginning. The show is educational, and if the products were to be educational too, they would need her input. The ancillary businesses offer a wonderful opportunity to extend the learning in the show and provide far transfer. Since the show is interactive, for example, the online service provided a perfect opportunity to build upon what was taught in the show in a way that was even more interactive because of the nature of the medium.

Once again, it had to be a collaborative effort and there had to be a respect and trust between research and all the lines of business. Research had to learn about each of the businesses, and the businesses had to learn what the experts know about *Blue's Clues* and child development and learning. One of research's primary roles was to ensure that *Blue's Clues* never became a logo-slapping brand, where quality and content take a back seat to simply putting a logo on ancillary products.

CLUES FOR Using Research in Business

Research is knowledge and knowledge is power, but it all depends on how you use it. In order for research to have the impact it is capable of having, decision makers have to think of it differently and researchers need to see themselves in a different light. Here are some suggestions for how you can make your product or service a phenomenon:

- Involve research in every phase of product development.

- Never assume you know your customer.

- Use research as a tool for helping you stay true to your mission and connected to your customer.

- Hold managers accountable for making decisions based on the facts.

- Don't skimp on research in lean times.

- Educate people on the value of research and show them how to use it.

- Encourage researchers to speak the language of the people they are trying to influence.

- Help build the research department's credibility by requiring its staff to always give the reasons why something can and can't be done.

- Involve research in creative problem solving.

- Use research to improve your product on a continuous basis and as a way of staying consciously competent.

- Use research on how customers feel about the product or service and how it affects them to motivate people in the organization.

CLUES FOR Using Research to Find Your Dream Job

Research is an invaluable tool when you are looking for a job—particularly when you are looking for the job that does more than provide you with a paycheck. In fact, in today's complex job market being a good researcher is a must.

Research goes beyond searching for jobs in the countless job boards on the Internet. One of the ways to land your dream job is to identify the company you want to work for first. Then get acquainted with that company so that when the right position opens up, you will be one of the "first in line" and someone the company is already familiar with. Plus, that company will be sure to appreciate your creative, strategic thinking.

So, assuming you know what you want to do and you have prepared yourself, the opportunites are there. You simply have to dig for them. Here's a list of resources for helping you research and find the job that is right for you:

- College alumni, alumni associations, and directories

- Professional and trade associations and directories

- Information from the Internet and other sources on companies and industries: articles, annual reports, corporate officers, products and services, office locations, mission and values statements, and so on

- Internet job sites

- Your own business and professional networks

- Groups and associations for women, minority groups, and the disabled

Publications are also a good resource. Here's a list of some you may want to consult:

- *Fortune*'s list of Most Admired Companies

- *Working Mother*'s list of Best Companies for Working Mothers

- Website Directories: CareerXRoads by Crispan and Mehler, MMC Group, Kendall, NJ 08824. <www.careerxroads.com> The Directory of Executive Recruiters 2001, Kennnedy Information, LLC, Fitzwilliam, NH 03447. <www.kennedyinfo .com>

- *Dun & Bradstreet's Million Dollar Directory*

- *Standard & Poor's Industry Survey*

- *Encyclopedia of Associations*

- *Entrepreneur* magazine

- The *Wall Street Journal, New York Times,* and local papers

- Bureau of Labor Statistics publications.

CHAPTER Summary

To keep the customer the focus of your organization, research must be an integral part of the decision-making process. If the people in research are doing their jobs, they should know what the customer thinks, wants, and feels better than anyone else in the company. In addition to playing a major role in defining the core product, Research should provide ongoing information and feedback about how the customer is responding to the product.

People and departments must be educated about the value of research in order for it to realize its potential impact and ensure that the company and departments are staying true to the mission and connected to the customer. Research professionals must be trained to give findings and feedback in ways that show respect and consideration for the needs of other departments. To be an effective part of the decision-making process, research profession- als must work with other departments as creative problem solvers. Researchers must speak in the language of the people they are trying to influence.

Clue #3

Research is the tool that keeps you connected to your customer and aligned with your mission. When you use research as the basis of your decision making, you will be able to meet the needs of your customer with amazing precision.

CHAPTER 4

Clue In to Your Technology and Workplace

USING TECHNOLOGY TO FULFILL THE MISSION

Companies today recognize that technology is a powerful and necessary tool that can dramatically impact a company's ability to compete in the marketplace. Few companies, however, use technology to its full advantage.

Some companies consistently spend huge sums of money on state-of-the-art equipment and software (much of which they don't need), but fail to train their people well enough to use it. Others have unrealistic expectations of technology—they try to get it to do things that should be done through other means. Still others allow the limitations of technology to limit their business—they are not creative enough in the way they apply it to business problems and solutions.

People make assumptions about what hardware and software can and can't do before they even test it out. They fall into the trap of making decisions about what to buy based on other peoples' recommendations, despite the fact that their needs may be very different. Another trap is being too goal-oriented when they are assessing technology. Instead of experimenting with it—the whole "innovation through play" idea—they decide what they want it to do and ask the "experts" if the technology can do it. They take the "experts'" word at face value without experimenting and finding out for themselves. Technology is a multifaceted tool. What one person does with a piece of software may be very different from what another person does—even if both are experts.

Nelson Torres, former freelance technical director for *Blue's Clues,* says, "Most business owners won't take the time to understand their technology or the technology that is out there so they have to make decisions about it on blind faith. They don't know enough to be able to discern if they have a good technical consultant or not. If they don't have at least a working knowledge of their technology, they can't be a part of the problem-solving process."

From the beginning, the *Blue's Clues* creators knew that technology would play a major role in the fulfillment of their mission. One of the reasons *Blue's Clues* is such a breakthrough show is because of the breakthroughs they made in technology. They actually invented a production process, which, along with the show's design, enabled them to produce something that looked totally different from anything else on television.

The process also enabled them to produce episodes at a far lower cost and in a much shorter time than they would have been able to do using conventional methods. It takes about 16 weeks for an overseas company to animate one 22-minute show. In contrast, it takes *Blue's Clues* about eight weeks to animate *two* 24-minute shows.

The story of how they did it is another powerful example of what a small group of people can achieve when they have a clear mission and vision; when they refuse to let obstacles stand in the way of their mission; and when they work collaboratively, each contributing his or her own unique piece, respecting one another, and listening and learning from one another, to come up with solutions to otherwise impossible situations and obstacles.

THE CHALLENGE

When Angela Santomero, Traci Paige Johnson, and Todd Kessler created the show, they knew its look and visual design would be integral to the attachment children would have to the show. Traci had designed it so that it would be warm and inviting ("yummy"), and so that it would make sense to preschoolers, which is why she used everyday, familiar materials—paper, clay, and pipe cleaners. The objects she uses are recognizable to preschoolers because they are already a part of a preschooler's world. The familiar objects help to create a comfortable, understandable universe for them.

Instead of using puppets and traditional animation like most children's television shows, she used simple cutout shapes and a vivid array of textures and colors to make it reminiscent of a children's storybook—a storybook that looks like it could just as easily have been designed by preschoolers themselves. Her hope was that it would be so inviting that they would want to reach out and touch the television screen.

Traci's cutout style was easily adapted to animation but they knew traditional methods would be too costly. The creators knew they wanted to produce the show with desktop computers and inexpensive software, but there was a problem: it had never been done before. All of the production experts they interviewed to produce the pilot said it was impossible to produce a 24-minute television series on regular Macintosh desktop computers. Nickelodeon, the *Blue's Clues* creators, and a company called Big Pink were about to prove them wrong.

LUCK OR DESTINY

How the people and the cutting-edge technology came together in such a perfect way—just like so many other pieces of the *Blue's Clues* story—leads one to believe in destiny. The creators knew they wanted to do the show on desktop computers, but they had no idea how to do it. They searched for someone with the technological background to make it happen and found John La Sala and Lisa Overton, owners and partners of the production company Big Pink. The company specialized in producing television commercials, but the creators believed they had the knowledge they needed to invent a whole new process.

At the time, John was teaching a class on two-dimensional animation using Photoshop and After Effects software, which he used at Big Pink in creating commercials for clients such as Jeep and General Electric. As fate would have it, in his class at the time was a young student by the name of Dave Palmer, who was working on his masters degree in film animation. Although barely out of school, Dave would provide one of the major keys to producing the show on desktop computers, and he would eventually become a key part of the *Blue's Clues* team.

At New York University, a majority of Dave's classes revolved around traditional animation methods, which employed drawings on paper or clay or paint on glass and were shot with a film camera. When Dave took John's class, he had no particular goal in mind—the computer was just another animation tool, which he wanted to add to his toolbox of software knowledge.

While learning and experimenting with the software that was being taught in the class, Dave was working on his thesis, a film in which he used a more traditional animation process involving pencil drawings transferred to sheets of clear acetate, called *cels*, and then painted. It was a process similar to that used by most children's television shows and animated features.

When the majority of television shows are produced with traditional cel animation techniques, the writing, storyboarding, scene layouts, and primary animation drawings are done in the U.S. The drawings that go between the primary drawings are done overseas in countries such as Korea, India, and Vietnam. Although there is a significant cost savings by shipping the work overseas, the process is still time consuming and expensive, especially when you consider that the traditional animation process requires 12 to 24 drawings per second to simulate fluid motion. This means that thousands of drawings can be required for a 30-minute television show, depending on the style of animation.

There's nothing more beautiful than a nicely drawn and painted animation cel, but traditional animation has its limitations. Dust can get on the lens of the camera or on the cels while you are shooting. Cels can be mistakenly stacked in the wrong order by the camera person. Or an animator could find after viewing the processed film that a light shifted halfway through a long shooting session, requiring the sequence to be totally reshot.

When drawing on paper as in a traditional animation method, once pen is put to paper, making changes to the performance can be time consuming. If, for example, an artist draws a three-second sequence, about 30 to 40 drawings of someone swinging his or her arm overhead, and realizes after the sequence has been shot that the arc of the arm is wrong, the artist has to redraw all or part of the entire sequence from scratch to correct the motion. Different styles of traditionally drawn animation require more or fewer drawings, but one thing they all have in common is that it takes a lot of time to complete the drawings.

While experiencing all the limitations of traditional animation as he completed his thesis film, Dave was experimenting with Photoshop and After Effects in John La Sala's class. As he was playing around with the software, he created successive drawings that, when viewed in order, looked like a walking panther. He drew the animation on paper, scanned it into the computer, and colored it in Photoshop. He then drew a big long background, scanned that into the computer, and painted it in PhotoShop as well. Next, he brought the animation and the background into After Effects, put the background behind the character, and ran the animation while he moved the background behind the character. It was like the traditional animation setup, except without

Cel animation requires an average of 15 individual cels, or images, per second. If *Blue's Clues* used this method (demonstrated here by Animation Director Dave Levy), one episode would require thousands of cels, all drawn, inked, and painted by hand. (photo by Gallucci Imaging, Inc.)

Animation Director Dale Clowdis uses a desktop computer to animate a scene. Desktop animation enables a team of ten *Blue's Clues* animators to animate two 24-minute episodes in about eight weeks, far faster than more traditional methods. (photo by Gallucci Imaging, Inc.)

the lights, the film camera, the cels, the dust, and the long shooting times. The computer did the "shooting" for him while he did other things.

Dave didn't know it at the time, but he had just made a discovery that would have a huge impact on the show. He was also a terrific animator, so when Big Pink agreed to produce the *Blue's Clues* pilot, John asked Dave to work with him and Lisa on it.

GEARING UP FOR THE PILOT

During the summer of 1995, John, Lisa, and Dave worked with the *Blue's Clues* creators to develop the technological and production process that was fundamental to fulfilling the mission of the show. Despite being a seasoned video and film producer, John had never had a client quite like *Blue's Clues*. They were so young and they had modest production experience, but they didn't let that stop them from wanting to push the technological envelope.

Dave believed in the show from the beginning and had an instant chemistry with the creators. He was impressed by the fact that they cared so much about producing a high-quality show that was good for kids. He especially liked that they didn't want to talk down to kids. They wanted to create a sophisticated, edgy show void of the cutesy, syrupy stuff so often found in children's television shows. He loved Traci's fun, simple, cutout style. Most of all, he liked their collaborative style of working.

At meetings, the creators would ask John, Lisa, and Dave, "Can you do this?" "Can you do that?" Dave, who had little or no authority at the time, would impulsively reply, "Sure, we can do that." Dave confesses today that he had no idea how they would do it; he just knew in his heart it could be done. As Traci often says, "Leap and the net will follow."

John, Dave, and Lisa took the leap, and sure enough the net was there. It was the combination of their skills and the fortuitous and timely improvements in After Effects, the cutting-edge software, that allowed them to accomplish their goal. They went against conventional thinking and they succeeded. They found a way to produce a national television series with relatively inexpensive Macintosh computers, using inexpensive software that could be bought at any local computer store.

The process they developed enabled them to produce the pilot and hit the ground running when the show started production in January 1996. For you techies, here are the basics of the process they developed to produce the show. They shoot the live-action host against a blue screen on video (today, they shoot on digital video). The live-action footage is then sent to the Nickelodeon Digital Animation studio, where an editor brings the footage into a digital file with Media100 software. The blue background in front of which the live actor performs is removed with Ultimatte software.

One of the goals in developing the process was to make the show look as though it wasn't created in the computer but was freshly cut and put together with construction paper and clay. The art department makes everything by hand in miniature: drawers of tiny clothes, furniture, and the characters themselves. To create the effect, the textures are exaggerated. The art department is a preschooler's dream. The physical space is an explosion of felt, construction paper, and clay.

After the elements are made, they are shot into the computer with a digital camera so low-tech becomes high-tech. After all the elements are shot with the camera, the digital design department puts the background and characters together. The digital designers are the architects of the world of *Blue's Clues*. The environment is kept organic by using Photoshop to create dropshadows and "yummify" all the elements. The performances of the animated characters are then created with After Effects, which is also used to marry the animation with the background and live action.

They not only created a process that looked just like traditional cutout animation, but the process they developed was incredibly flexible and faster. With their process, they could make changes instantly. It allowed them to take input research was obtaining from the kids and change it on the spot. *Blue's Clues* takes about 12 weeks to completely animate four episodes (about an hour and a half of animation). Using a more traditional method, it could take weeks or months to animate just one character in a two-minute scene. The *Blue's Clues* process was not only faster and less expensive, but because Dave set up the pilot so that a library of documents would be created—documents that would be added to with each episode and used over and over again—over time it would take less and less time to animate episodes.

THE PERSONAL STORY

A s an animator I am an actor whose job it is to bring characters to life. Like most actors, I have an affinity for the characters I create—some more than others. One of the most fascinating things about my experience at Blue's Clues *has been my relationship with Blue.*

I remember when Traci gave me her flat cutout design of Blue and asked me to adapt the design so it could be animated, I was anxious. I wanted to stay true to Traci's design but I knew I would have to put some of myself into Blue's character. I knew how she should move and bark and act, and I knew she had to be able to carry a television series over many seasons worth of shows. So I aimed to create an engaging, loveable, fully developed character with a lot of emotion.

From the beginning, Blue's goals were to have fun, teach kids, and to learn. She was to be an inquisitive character who already knew a lot and was excited about learning. She was to be a preschooler who looked like a puppy. I knew on paper who she was supposed to be but it was still my job to bring her to life—to give her her personality.

One of the first things I did was make a list of the multitude of things she would have to be able to do—things like spin in place, hop, and bark—and then I started to animate her. The more I animated her, the more I grew to love the character. I noticed that I got frustrated when I watched someone else draw or animate her when they didn't seem to get who she was. It's not unusual for an animator to develop an attachment to a character they are animating because you put so much of yourself into them. I guess that's why some of my friends say that Blue reminds them of me.

When the creators of the show asked me to join the production company full-time after I worked on the pilot, I knew it was a place I could do creative work that would last and make a difference, but it was perhaps Blue who had the biggest influence in my decision. I felt like I knew her personality, her shape, her character as well as I knew myself, and I wanted to make sure she was taken care of. I wanted to make sure that she grew into the puppy I had intended her to be. Today Blue is animated by some of the best animators in the industry so I know she's in great hands, but I still keep a watchful eye over her.

Dave Palmer
Supervising Animation Director/Producer

SAVING TIME AND MONEY

One of the myths in many companies is that more expensive is always better—the more your technology costs, the more effectively it will serve the business. As mentioned previously, *Blue's Clues* is produced on inexpensive desktop computers with inexpensive software you can buy at any local computer store. That's a substantial savings when you consider there are 35 to 40 animators, designers, and editors, each with his or her own computer stations.

The logical assumption most people would make is that inexpensive equipment would produce a less than superior product, but the people at *Blue's Clues* don't make assumptions; they question everything. They also save money by combining high-tech with low-tech. The show is produced with inexpensive, everyday art supplies such as clay, pipe cleaners, construction paper, and so forth. And while many productions farm much of their work outside, *Blue's Clues* does everything in-house.

One reason companies become frustrated with their technology is because they don't plan well enough the activities surrounding its use and then they blame the technology when tasks and objectives cannot be accomplished on schedule. At *Blue's Clues,* they spend a tremendous amount of time in preplanning. Every preproduction meeting is geared toward nailing down as many decisions as possible before production begins, especially before they begin the time-consuming, expensive part of the production such as the live-action shoot, art and design, digital design, and animation. By planning well and controlling the controllable, they are much better able to deal with the unexpected.

One of the advantages of working digitally is that it keeps the production fluid; changes can be made quickly and easily. For example, if an object created by the art department isn't working in a scene because its color is clashing with something else or because its color isn't saturated enough and the object can't be seen clearly, the artist usually doesn't have to remake the object. Instead, the digital designer working on the scene can quickly alter the object's color digitally until it works.

Without digital technology, changes to painted backgrounds would have to be repainted from scratch. Since all the animators, artists, researchers, designers, etc., are in-house, whoever needs to see the changes can do so at the designer's desk. The color can be easily changed again and again until it works for everyone.

One of the greatest benefits of working digitally, of course, is that changes from research can be made easily and quickly. Customer feedback can be put into the system almost instantly. Animation, art, and digital design stay in close contact with research to ensure that they are getting the information they need on a timely basis.

USING TECHNOLOGY CREATIVELY

Many companies are slaves to their technology because they don't know how to work with it creatively. Instead of viewing it as a tool, as a means to an end, they see it as the end. They fail to experiment with, get to know, or be creative with the technology. And they fail to acknowledge that the people using the tool are far more valuable than the tool itself. The people in the company do the work, not the computers.

It's interesting that *Blue's Clues* is a computer-generated show produced by the computer generation for a generation for whom the computer will play an even larger role in their lives. When they were developing the production process for the show, Dave and some of the others on the team would play with the software for hours on end. They experimented with it without any particular goal in mind, just to see what it could do. A lot of their innovations came as a result of pure play. For those of us who didn't grow up with computers, our fear of it, or perhaps our fear of our own limitations, keeps us from relating to it creatively. The computer is just a tool, like a pencil, a calculator, or a hammer.

Blue's Clues has such a unique look not just because of the software but because of how the software is used. One of the goals in developing the process was to make the show look as though it had been produced using the traditional animation process. One of the true tests was whether an outside animator could tell if it was produced on the computer.

When they started developing the process, they knew the computer had a downside when it comes to animation. It has a tendency to create slow, smooth, and robotic movement, which results in a "floaty" look, devoid of any real weight to what is being animated, which is certainly not the look they wanted. Dave and the other animators still have to wrestle with the computer to create real and natural-looking movements. They had to apply the principles of traditional animation to the digital process in order to get the final product to look like traditional animation.

Animators are actors, and traditional animation is an art that employs the principles of timing, composition, exaggeration, and so on, to tell a story, convey emotion, and create a personality. Computers are not actors—they are simply a tool through which the animator expresses his or her art.

The animation process used in *Blue's Clues* actually provides animators with greater opportunity to be creative. They actually get to act. Often in a traditional animation studio, a director will give the animator what is called an exposure sheet—a frame-by-frame guide for a scene that tells the animator, for example, in what frame the character should blink or in what frame the character should wave his hand.

With the *Blue's Clues* process, animators are given acting direction similar to how live-action directors work with actors. An animator, for example, is told where the character enters, what kind of mood the character is in, where and when he interacts with another character, when the character changes moods, when he exits, and so on. The animator's job is to work out the timing and look of the whole scene: the character's body posture, glances, reactions, and the way the character walks and moves. Animators are given an enormous amount of information up front about who the character is and the goals of the scene. As long as animators stay in character and true to the story, they can be as creative as they wish.

From the beginning, the digital designers and animators were careful to use the computer only for what it could do best. This was difficult for some who were so focused on the software and what it could do. For example, with the computer they can make a three-dimensional chair and then rotate it so it can be seen from all sides. Instead, the art and design department makes a miniature chair out of clay and takes a picture of each side with a digital camera. The result is a much better chair because it looks handmade and organic, with imperfections the computer chair doesn't have.

ASTONISHING THE SOFTWARE PROVIDERS

As Dave, John, and Lisa were developing the process for the show, they knew they were pushing the Macintosh computer to its limit. They also knew they had pushed the envelope with the software. Years later, when *Blue's Clues* was in full production, Adobe, the makers of Photoshop and After Effects, learned how the software was being used. They couldn't believe that an animated series was being produced for a television network with their software. Not even the developers of the software knew it could be used to create character animation on the scale *Blue's Clues* was using it.

Adobe was so impressed that they asked *Blue's Clues* to be a part of their client development group, which works to constantly improve Adobe products. Not only did Adobe benefit, but so did *Blue's Clues*. Adobe made numerous changes and improvements in the software based on *Blue's Clues* input, which made the *Blue's Clues* process even faster and enabled them to create an even better show.

The moral of the story? Play with the software you are using. See what it can do without any particular goal in mind. If you are doing something interesting with a piece of software or you have an idea for an improvement, let the software provider know. If they are an enlightened company like Adobe, they will probably welcome your input.

ANOTHER FIRST

Fast-forward to 1999, two years after the show's premiere. The show is a huge success. There are now 20 animators, 11 digital designers, and 5 art directors and model makers working with Dave on the show. They continuously work to improve the process, but there are problems with it.

When the show started production, everyone worked very long hours to produce enough episodes to meet the programming schedule requirements. They were passionate about what they were doing and often worked a 60- to 70-hour week. They had some of the best and fastest computers available at the time, but they were pushing them and themselves in order to complete the first few episodes.

Before the show was a hit, the production was housed in temporary space where the animators worked in a big room on a bunch of scattered desks in a long row. There was no particular organization to their work space, so time was wasted just getting work from department to department.

It was difficult enough finding the right people to work on the show. There weren't many people who knew traditional animation and who also knew computer animation. Today, animators who work on *Blue's Clues* have almost celebrity status, but before the show became a mega-hit, there weren't a lot of animators who were interested in working in a simple style with cutouts on a Macintosh computer. Most young animators wanted to draw for Disney or work on animated features. There also weren't a lot of schools that had programs that included traditional animation skills with computer skills—it was usually one or the other.

Nickelodeon's solution to the problem was a $6 million digital animation studio, which was one of the first of its kind. Building the studio, which today houses 140 people including 70 animators, was an enormous undertaking—again, they had no model to use as a guide. They were once again in uncharted territory. It was a significant capital outlay, but as Chris Linn, Nickelodeon's vice president of productions operations, said, "Nickelodeon has never been about grinding out half hours of television programming. We had created a breakthrough, revolutionary program so we had to provide a workplace that would allow us to attract the best talent, keep them safe and happy, and provide them with the tools they needed to produce a high-quality show."

The first step was to hire an ergonomic specialist to evaluate the space and at the same time educate the animators about working habits such as posture, hand movements, and use of their eyes. The design and building of the studio was another collaborative effort. Nickelodeon's planning and design department and production technology department worked closely with the producers to create a studio that would meet the needs of *Blue's Clues*.

The animators and designers themselves gave a tremendous amount of input into the design. Chris and the Nickelodeon group who designed the studio spent endless hours with the animators, talking to them about how they did their work and what they felt they needed to be comfortable and do their work most efficiently. Nickelodeon was committed to creating a studio that was logistically efficient and totally customized to the process and the mission of the show.

The studio, which became a showcase for Nickelodeon, required the construction of a huge infrastructure: supplemental power, supplemental air, and special lighting. The design of the hydraulic desks alone took months to complete. The work space was laid out according to the work flow, and the customized workstations were designed several times before Nickelodeon signed off on the furniture. A button on the front of each computer desk raises and lowers the large screen monitor so that animators can work sitting or standing. All of the workstations are networked so that animators can trade files with each other and with other departments in seconds. Even the lighting was carefully planned to cut down on the glare on the monitors.

Nickelodeon had not only built a state-of-the-art studio, but they sent a loud message to the entire production. It said they believed in them. And the way they listened to and worked with the animators in designing the studio said they respected them and cared what they thought. To this day, animators still feel free to call Chris and offer suggestions for how the facility can be further improved.

USING TECHNOLOGY TO EXTEND YOUR REACH

Blue's Clues uses technology to accomplish their mission in other ways as well. They use it every opportunity they can to strengthen their relationship with their customers. *Blue's Clues* CD-ROMs and the Nick Jr. Web site, which are discussed in greater detail in Chapter 6, allow preschoolers to interact even more than they do with the show. The use of technology outside the show enables *Blue's Clues* to do an even better job of empowering, challenging, and building the self-esteem of preschoolers while making them laugh.

CLUES FOR Using Technology in Business

Here are some guidelines for making sure your company gets the maximum benefit from the technology you purchase:

- Be clear about what you want your technology to do.

- Stay current with your equipment and software, but resist the temptation to spend enormous sums of money updating your technology every time something new comes out. Make

THE AUDIENCE SPEAKS

The following message and reply appeared on the Nick Jr. Web site message board for parents and viewers other than preschoolers:

BLUE'S CLUES IS THE BEST!!

   Hey all! I am 14 years old and I LOVE *Blue's Clues!* I think that it is the coolest cartoon in the world. Blue and her friends are so cute! I just love the show so very much!

RE: *BLUE'S CLUES* IS THE BEST!!

   Don't feel bad that you're over the age of nine and love *Blue's Clues*. My entire dorm room at college is decked out in *Blue's Clues!* It's so much fun to be a kid!

sure you are fully using the capabilities of your current technology.

- Don't overspend when buying equipment when simpler is better, but at the same time buy equipment that is a little more powerful than you need so you have some room to grow.

- Encourage people to think of technology simply as a tool— as a means to an end instead of the end itself.

- Make sure you give people the training they need to make maximum use of available technology.

- If your technology is doing the job, keep it. If it isn't working, don't be afraid to toss it.

- Don't use the computer for things that can best be done through other means.

- Encourage people to be creative with the technology they are given—encourage them to experiment and play with it—innovation will come through play!

- Never let your technology serve as an excuse for not meeting your business objectives or fulfilling your mission.

- Be the master of your technology, not a slave to it.

CLUES FOR Using Technology in Your Personal Life

The same principles apply for personal use. Here are a few more:

- If you are not computer-literate, find a way to develop your skills. In today's marketplace, computer literacy can make an enormous difference in your career.

- If you have blocks about using the computer, find an expert or someone who at least knows more than you do, who can sit with you and help you get comfortable with it.

- Ask friends who use the computer extensively to tell you the various ways they use it to save time and accomplish personal goals, even though their goals may be different from yours. Resolve to learn how you can use it to improve your life.

- Keep adding to your knowledge of different kinds of software programs.

- Don't let the computer rule your life or detract from your relationships.

CHAPTER Summary

Companies need to be clear about what they want their technology to do. They need to guard against trying to get their technology to solve problems that can best be solved in other ways. One of the ways to get the maximum benefit from available technology is to experiment with it to see what it can and can't do. Users should not assume that hardware or software can't do something because someone else said it can't. Technology should be applied creatively and with flexibility.

Technology should be viewed as a tool to be used in service of the company's business objectives. Companies should never be a slave to their technology. Technology that no longer serves the company's business needs should be tossed, but only after it has been thoroughly tested and examined to see what it can and can't do. One of the biggest mistakes many companies make is to buy expensive, state-of-the-art technology that they don't need, or to fail to train people properly to use it.

Clue #4

When you are the master of your **technology** and you use it creatively to accomplish your business objectives, it can empower you to do things for your customer that no one else has done.

CHAPTER 5

Clue In to Your Work Processes

BUILDING THE ORGANIZATION

If you have ever worked in a start-up operation, you know it can be both exhilarating and exhausting. Everyone does everything. Roles are not defined. Few processes or systems are in place, but energy output is extremely high and people are committed. Everyone works long hours just to get the product out the door.

What we have just described is one of the primary reasons the majority of small businesses fail in the first 18 months. They fail because they don't spend time putting the organizational foundations in place. They may have a great product, but they don't have an organization through which they can efficiently and effectively produce and deliver the product.

In its simplest terms, building an organization is about developing the proper relationships between the work, the people, and the workplace. The disciplines inherent in that process enable leaders to harness and focus the organization's energy. Without these disciplines, it's virtually impossible for a company to meet its business goals and objectives. The energy and commitment everyone feels in the beginning can quickly disintegrate into chaos and frustration when the disciplines are absent. It's fertile ground for interpersonal conflicts because there is so much work but no agreement as to *how* the work is to get done.

When the *Blue's Clues* creators presented the pilot to Nickelodeon in the summer of 1995, they were told to begin production immediately. The show had the complete support of Nickelodeon President Herb Scannell. It was to premiere in September 1996, at which time they were to have ten episodes completed. It was a monumental task.

The creators were about to be stretched as they never had been before. It's one thing to come up with a terrific idea for a children's television show and quite another to put the show into production. At the time, they had few resources, no infrastructure or system for doing anything, and little management experience. None of them had ever started a show or a business from scratch.

Chris Linn, Nickelodeon's vice president of productions operations, helped with the business side of the production—financial planning, securing resources, and so on—while Janice Burgess, vice president of productions for Nick Jr., shepherded the show through the network. The creators, however, still needed someone on their immediate team who shared and could execute their creative vision—someone who could take the rough pilot and turn it into a professional business. They needed someone with not only a good business mind but someone who could translate the vision into a sustainable television series—someone who could fuse the creative with the production.

To get the production up and running, there were thousands of tasks and details to be planned for and accomplished—everything from hiring people, to organizing the workspace, to creating the production schedule, to managing the budget. The person for the job was Jennifer Twomey, a young producer who had wanted desperately to work in children's television. Like the rest of the creators, it was as though she had been preparing for her golden career opportunity her entire life. Her unique combination of talents was precisely what the creators needed. She was strategic in her thinking. She was a take-charge person, a natural leader with a strong creative side. Not only was she inventive in the way she got around obstacles and set up the production, but she would go on to be a writer for the series and use her creative talents to produce CD-ROMs, albums, and even storybooks for *Blue's Clues*. The creators had found themselves another whole-brain thinker.

In the first four months after the pilot was approved, Jen and the three creators worked into the wee hours of the morning every day, putting together plans for virtually everything—from the details of the show itself, to the processes and systems for producing the show, to the creation of the work environment and culture. Together, they put the bones of the production in place.

After the show was in production the first year, it was obvious that Jen's talents could be better used to work with the creators in ongoing strategic planning and in translating the *Blue's Clues* vision into the ancillary businesses. There was so much interfacing and negotiating that had to be done with other parts of Nickelodeon that she couldn't handle the day-to-day details of the production and do the strategic work at the same time. The show was growing in popularity and becoming much more sophisticated, which meant the fundamental processes and systems initially put in place were no longer sufficient. *Blue's Clues* had outgrown the organizational structure that had brought it to stardom. Like a snake that had outgrown its skin, it was time to reorganize and refine what Jen and the creators had so carefully put in place.

At the time, Wendy Harris had been freelancing on the show as assistant director. The creators had noticed how skillful she was at managing people and moving work through the production process. There are some people who have a natural ability to organize. Their minds are like computers when it comes to figuring out the who, what, where, when, and why of a very complex job involving large numbers of people with different sets of objectives and needs. Like an orchestra leader, they are able to get people to work in harmony to accomplish the end result. Their ability to juggle a lot of balls at one time and keep their eye on every detail is a gift. It's a way of thinking that can't be taught. You either have it or you don't. Wendy had it in spades. She was able to create magic.

The creators asked Wendy to come on board full-time as the show's producer. The work and production processes were in need of a total overhaul, which is what Wendy set out to do. Although she was familiar with parts of the process, she approached the task like a scientist, making no assumptions.

THE KEY TO HIGH PERFORMANCE AND EFFICIENCY

Managers and employees everywhere today bemoan the fact that they don't have enough people to get the work done. We have a workforce that is on the verge of burnout. Companies try to save money by laying people off, which leaves the already stressed-out survivors feeling exploited and taxed to the limit.

The irony is that much of the work the workers are performing adds little or no value to begin with. Too often, companies have the resources they need to get the job done, but the organization's work processes obstruct rather than facilitate the movement of work through the system.

One of the reasons *Blue's Clues* is a success is that their work processes are sophisticated and continuously refined based on input from the people doing the work. There is also a strong marriage between creative and production. The work and creative processes are so inextricably linked that it is hard to tell where one ends and the other begins. Of course, getting to that place was no small task. It took a good two years and a lot of mistakes before they had a system that served the product the way it needed to be served.

When Wendy and the executive producers redesigned the *Blue's Clues* production process, they knew they could never lose sight of the fact that they were producing a creative product. Everything production did would have to be done with the vision in mind. They also knew they would have to design work processes, which would do the following:

- Empower people and departments to produce a high-quality product in a timely manner.

- Demonstrate respect for the needs of each department.

- Protect those departments at the end of the process so their work wasn't rushed due to missed deadlines of those departments before them in the process.

- Provide "shock absorbers" for unexpected events and uncontrollable factors.

- Allow for flexibility.

Most of all, they wanted to design a work process that would free people rather than enslave them. The system should be in service of the end product—it should not be an end in itself.

always loved the world of arts and entertainment. As far back as I can remember, whenever I went to a play, a movie, or the ballet, I sat on the edge of my seat with pure excitement. Of course, I couldn't wait for the experience to begin, but I also wanted so much to be a part of it. Although I took ballet for ten years, loved movies and museums, put on plays, and fantasized about being an actress, my dream of having a career in entertainment stayed just that— a fantasy.

Like many people, I was influenced by the expectations and wishes others had of me. Coming from a family of successful professionals and businesspeople, I never felt that a career in the arts was "legitimate." After I graduated from undergraduate school with a degree in psychology, rather than get my MBA and pursue a more traditional career in business, I decided to move to Paris. Although I had no job and didn't speak the language, it was oddly one of the easiest decisions I have ever made. It was just something I had to do.

For two years, while working all kinds of jobs in Paris, I immersed myself in the arts. Away from friends and family and other influences and expectations, I felt free to consider what I wanted for my life and career. I was finally able to acknowledge what I truly wanted to do rather than what I thought I should do. It was there that I decided I would pursue a career in entertainment.

Finally acknowledging what I wanted to do, I attended film school and worked as a freelancer on a number of productions, which eventually led me to Blue's Clues. *My job at* Blue's Clues *has given me the wonderful opportunity to not only use my production skills but to be creative and to be a part of something I believe in. Now what I enjoy most about what I do at* Blue's Clues *is that I imagine some kids sitting on the edge of their seat with excitement, waiting to see something that I was a part of making.*

To me, life is a process. I've learned that when you listen to your heart and follow your own dreams, you allow yourself to be open to life and all of its amazing opportunities.

Wendy Harris
Supervising Producer

STEPS TO CREATING EFFECTIVE WORK PROCESSES

Designing effective work processes is like putting together a giant jigsaw puzzle, particularly when there are a lot of steps in the process and a lot of people and departments involved. In many companies, each department develops its own work processes with little or no concern for the needs and timing requirements of the other departments in the process. They have little or no understanding of what other departments do, what it takes for them to do what they do, and how each impacts the other.

Cross-functional teams were originally designed to get everyone in a process working together to accomplish the end result rather than each department focusing solely on their piece of the process. The system Wendy and the executive producers designed actually became one of the vehicles for transforming the *Blue's Clues* production group into a true cross-functional team. Here are the seven steps they took in designing the process:

1. **Study the big picture.** The first thing Wendy did was to study the overall product, in this case the show, and the technology that was used to produce it. She worked her way back from the end result or overall objective and asked herself what the major steps were in the process.

2. **Gain an understanding of what each department does.** She sat with each department and asked them to educate her on what they did, how they did it, and what they needed to do their work. She knew it would be impossible to design an effective work process unless she had a full appreciation of what each department did and what they needed. If people were to own the system she designed, she knew they would need to have input into it.

3. Break the process into steps—create a map. After doing her research, she laid out all of the pieces and created a flowchart or map of the sequences of tasks that had to be accomplished to get to the end result.

4. Assess pitfalls and frustrations. After getting the basic flow of the work, she went back to each department for more in-depth discussions about their work. She asked each department what was working for them and what was not working. With that information, she fine-tuned the map or flowchart she had developed and refined the time frames in the process.

5. Identify checkpoints in the process. Wendy and her associates looked at the entire process and determined key steps that would be used to assess their progress and how well they were doing in meeting the schedule. This way, they could address scheduling problems in a timely manner, before it was too late.

6. Present the process and get ownership. After completing the process, Wendy presented it to each department and as she did, she educated them on what every other department did and what they needed to do their jobs. She also educated them on the rationale behind the process, particularly when one or more of their requests could not be met. She asked them for their feedback and tweaked the process once again. And last, she asked if they could commit to the process. By approving the process, they were holding themselves accountable to follow it.

7. Constantly monitor and refine the process. At the end of each season, each department sits down with Wendy and/or her associate producers and evaluates how well the system worked. They constantly refine the process as the team and show evolves, eliminating or adding steps as needed. Issues and problems that

arise are studied to determine if they are a fault of the process or if they occur due to some other reason. If it was a fault of the process, the process is changed. If it wasn't, the issue and how it was resolved is documented and filed for future reference in the event the issue comes up again.

Although it was another long, hard struggle getting there, the benefits that came from the refined system were enormous. It was like cleaning house. It eliminated a lot of inefficiencies and old baggage. As they continuously monitor and refine the process, the benefits continue to grow. The system is so refined now that they hardly need it. Here's what the refined process did and continues to do for the people and the product:

- Since people felt heard, they felt respected. They felt their needs were addressed, so they were more inclined to be sensitive to the needs of others.

- In understanding the process, each department had a better understanding and appreciation for what the other departments did and what they needed, facilitating a much greater sense of team.

- The efficiency of the process took much of the stress out of the work. People were able to be more creative with their work and to enjoy the process. The show is about helping preschoolers have fun as they learn, something that is more likely to happen when the people producing the show are having fun.

- There is little or no blaming, because the process works smoothly and people have what they need to do their jobs. People and departments take greater ownership and responsibility.

- People and departments have greater control over their work and their time. They aren't constantly working in crisis mode, which causes people to feel out of control.

- Fewer meetings are needed, because the work process clearly defines the decision-making process. Because the process breeds trust and respect, people don't feel they will be treated unfairly or taken advantage of if they don't attend every meeting.

- Because the system is so refined, it enables departments to be highly flexible and to respond quickly to changes and new projects.

THE ART OF APPLYING THE PROCESS

Any process, of course, is only as good as its application. If we lived in a perfect world, a process would always do what it was designed to do. In order for a process to work, it has to be constantly monitored. At *Blue's Clues,* Wendy and her associate producers are always scanning the process, assessing needs and problems, and either speeding up or slowing down the work of various departments so that the work flow stays fairly even and no one department feels dumped on or is left with little or nothing to do. They are constantly troubleshooting, asking people and departments if they have any issues or concerns.

Sometimes task-oriented, process-focused people become so fixed on the process itself that they lose perspective. In their rigid application of the process, they work against the product and the overall goals. Applying the process is an art. You have to dance with it. You have to be flexible and improvise, particularly when you are producing a creative product.

THE AUDIENCE SPEAKS

Dear *Blue's Clues*,

I sent an e-mail to *Blue's Clues* two years ago about my daughter, Molly. She is blind and has mild cerebral palsy, and *Blue's Clues* is her favorite show. She is almost five now, and when she hears the music she says, "Blue's Clues!" She has most of the shows memorized to the point that she can repeat what the characters are going to say before they say it. She even sings along with the songs in the most angelic voice.

She has been to the Live Show and had a fabulous time. I want to thank you from the bottom of my heart for creating such a wonderful show. Your show has helped my daughter in so many amazing ways that I don't think there is any way I can truly thank you enough. I hope you continue to make shows that help more children the way you have helped mine.

Thank you,

Lori Martin

DECISION-MAKING AND WORK PROCESSES

In order for work processes to flow smoothly and achieve the desired results, departments and individuals must have a clear understanding of their roles, responsibilities, and decision-making authority. When *Blue's Clues* first geared up for production, they fell into the trap that a lot of small businesses fall into. Virtually everyone, including the creators, attended almost every meeting. From the beginning, the creators wanted an inclusive work environment. They wanted people to feel they had a voice; they wanted them to feel empowered.

Initially, when the group was small, the all-inclusive decision-making process made people feel invested and important. They got to know one another and developed a strong sense of camaraderie. There were countless decisions to be made in the beginning, which meant a lot of meetings, but people were enjoying the process—for a while anyway. It wasn't long before the leaders learned that too much inclusivity can actually be a demotivator.

When everyone has to weigh in on every decision, work stalls and people become frustrated because it takes so long to get anything done. When everybody owns everything, no one owns anything. The people who have the expertise and whose area is most affected by the decision making are deflated. They are not able to do what they were hired to do. They don't have control over the work for which they are responsible.

How to find the balance—that was the challenge. The last thing they wanted was people and departments working in isolation. People had to collaborate. They had to make decisions with other people and departments in mind, but they had to find a way to do it more efficiently. And the creators had to let go. They had been attending most of the meetings and ultimately making most of the decisions. The people had the feeling of being empowered before because they had a voice but they actually weren't, because most of the decisions were being made by the leaders.

Once they realized their error, the creators wrestled with how to address the issue. They started by having fewer people go to meetings. Only those people directly affected by the meeting topic and consequent decisions would attend. At first, people saw it as a loss—they didn't have as much say in matters. Over time, however, they saw that they could be much more effective because they weren't spending all their time in meetings. And they had much more authority over the decisions that affected them.

It was a struggle finding the right balance, but today decision making at *Blue's Clues* is a very collaborative process. Because they have their work processes down to a fine science, they know exactly what decisions should be made when and by whom, and who needs to be advised of the decisions. The production process consists of more than 100 distinct steps. For each step, there is a goal or description. Some of the steps are meetings for the purpose of decision making. Most decisions are still made in group settings, because the work of the departments is so interconnected. The key, however, is in the work process design, making sure that the right people and departments are at the right meetings to make decisions—decisions which, if they aren't made correctly, can throw off the entire process and dramatically impact other departments down the line.

MEETINGS AND THE WORK PROCESS

If you have worked in a company or organization for any length of time, you know that meetings can be tremendous time wasters. Too often, the only thing decided at meetings is that there will be another meeting. And yet meetings are necessary to moving work through the system. Meetings are not the problem; the problem lies in how they are planned and managed.

At *Blue's Clues*, meetings are the forum for collaborative decision making, for ensuring that decisions aren't made by one department that are going to adversely affect another department. They are particularly used for creative problem solving. Here are some of the ways they ensure the efficiency and productivity of their meetings:

- Careful thought is always given to who should attend a meeting. In most cases, it is only those people who are affected by the decisions to be made at the meeting.

- There is always an appointed meeting leader.

- The meeting leader communicates to participants the goals of the meeting in advance.

- If participants are going to be asked to respond to something at the meeting, they are asked to think about it in advance (or review it if it is something to be reviewed) and give notes, concerns, and issues to the meeting leader in advance. The meeting leader uses the notes to develop the agenda. This way, meetings are used to address everyone's concerns.

- Meeting leaders ensure that only those items on the agenda are discussed.

- Decisions, action items, and next steps that come out of the meeting are summarized in writing and distributed to all meeting participants after the meeting.

One of the things they do to ensure that people who need approval from a number of departments are able to get it in a timely manner, is to block out time periods each week for certain kinds of meetings. People may not need the time slots, but if they do, they are assured that people won't be already booked at other meetings. Before establishing the weekly time slots, work was getting stalled because people were not available to give the sign-offs that allowed the work to move through the system.

USING OBSTACLES TO REFINE THE PROCESS

Anytime an organization experiences a major change, whether it's downsizing, doublesizing, a new product, or a restructuring, it's a perfect opportunity to refine the work processes. Any major change usually puts added stress on the people. Refining work processes can minimize the stress and help people feel better about the change, because it gives them something to focus on that they can control.

In 2000, *Blue's Clues* was such a hit that Nickelodeon asked the producers to double their production—they wanted more episodes coming out of the pipeline. The *Blue's Clues* senior staff was happy for the opportunity to grow, but at the same time they were apprehensive. After two years of refining their work processes and finally enjoying the benefits, they would now have to give it a complete overhaul. Just when the process had begun to hum they would have to go through the arduous task of developing a whole new system, and they would have to do it fast. They had to reconfigure the entire organization in a very short period in order to meet the schedule.

Blue's Clues was given the resources to do so, but doubling a company's staff still presents a host of challenges. People would have to be interviewed, hired, and trained. They would need to be immersed in the *Blue's Clues* way of doing things. The people heading the departments would have to find a way to get the same high-quality work out of two teams of people instead of one. The work space would have to be reconfigured. It was a major undertaking.

The senior staff knew that the increase in size could be an organizational nightmare if it wasn't presented properly to the staff, and carefully planned and orchestrated. Senior staff worked for weeks into the early hours of the morning, struggling with the challenge before them. One of the things they did was to study and scrutinize every single aspect of their work process. They particularly looked at paperwork flow—who got what when and whether it was even necessary. Once again, they looked at peoples' roles and further defined them. They looked at every person's job and every meeting—who attended them and who didn't. Every aspect of the process was up for questioning.

What is often a fiasco in most companies, leaving people totally confused and demoralized, actually turned into a positive for the organization and the people. There was enormous resistance and fear on the part of the staff in the beginning, but they soon learned that it was an opportunity to air their concerns about the present system and make things better.

Because there were more people to be managed, the department head positions were elevated. Leaders had to let go even more and empower people. And the work processes were so streamlined that productivity and efficiency increased dramatically. The *Blue's Clues* senior staff learned from that experience that what seems like insurmountable obstacles can be the best thing for an organization. They either destroy you or force you to be better.

CLUES FOR Improving Your Company's Work Processes

A company's work processes have a far-reaching impact on the people of an organization and the results they are able to achieve. Many companies keep working people harder and harder to get the work out the door but they stay in crisis mode because their work processes are outdated and ineffective. Designing, implementing, and refining a company's work processes requires an enormous commitment of time, but the payoff is huge. Effective work processes facilitate decision making, teamwork, trust, and respect among people and departments. They are fundamental to the fulfillment of a company's mission and the accomplishment of its goals and objectives. Here are some things to keep in mind as you design and refine your company's or team's work processes:

- Appoint a champion of your work processes—someone who understands the entire process, is a good organizer and manager, and is involved personally in the process.

- Always keep the mission and end goal in mind. Work processes should be in service of the product, not the other way around.

- Do a thorough study of your current process and interview key people from each department who are involved in the process. Find out what they do, how they do it, and what they need to do what they do.

- Assess each department's pitfalls and frustrations. Ask people where the snags in the process are for them.

- Break the process into steps and create a flowchart or map of how work should flow through the system.

- Gain commitment to the process from everyone involved in it. Ask them to review and critique the process once it is designed. Use their input to further refine it.

- Constantly monitor and refine the process. Evaluate each issue or problem that arises and determine if it is caused by the process. If so, change the process.

- Make sure someone who fully understands the process is constantly scanning it, assessing needs, and anticipating problems. Manage the process so that there is an even flow of work from department to department.

- Don't apply the process rigidly. Be flexible and don't be afraid to change it when necessary.

- Clearly define the roles, responsibilities, and decision-making authority of people and departments. Push decision making down to the appropriate level—make sure the right people and departments are involved in the appropriate decisions at the right time.

- Use meetings for collaborative decision making. Ask for input into the agenda from meeting participants in advance. Stick to the agenda and communicate the decisions, next steps, and action items to the appropriate people after the meeting.

- Use major changes or challenges within the organization as an opportunity to refine your work processes. Help people to see that they have more control than they think. They may not have control over what they do but they certainly can control how they do it.

CLUES FOR Streamlining Your Life

If you walk into some peoples' homes, it's obvious they have a place for everything. If you were to follow them for a week, you would find they have processes and systems for most of the repetitive tasks they perform in maintaining their life—like sorting the mail, paying bills, shopping for groceries, remembering birthdays, and so on. And then there are those whose home looks like a tornado hit it. Counters are cluttered. Many of the rooms look like there is a rummage sale in progress. Clothes are strewn from one end of the house to the other. If you were to follow them for a week, you would probably find that they have virtually no systems for doing anything.

Having systems and processes for your personal life can save a lot of time and headaches. It can also reduce stress and foster healthier, happier relationships. Processes help to make life run smoothly. They free you to concentrate on the important things in life. Here are some suggestions for helping your life run more smoothly by having better processes or systems:

- Assess for yourself and/or with the people you live with how well your life works in terms of your daily chores and life maintenance. Do you tend to be a "neat freak" on one extreme, totally disorganized on the other, or somewhere in between?

- Make a list of your goals and what is important to you. Ask your partner and family members or the people you live with to do the same.

- If you are a compulsive organizer, don't read the bullets that follow. Do, however, ask yourself if you are a slave to your systems. Can you relax if things are not totally organized— if things don't always flow perfectly? If not, practice being more flexible with your systems. Think about your life priorities. Is your compulsion for organization detracting from your relationships with other people? Are you driving yourself too hard?

- Make a list of the repetitive things you do to maintain your life. If you have a family or live with a group of people, look at how the entire family or group functions.

- For each item on the list, ask yourself if there is a system or process for performing it. If so, does it work? Ask yourself how it could be done better.

- If you have a family or live with a group of people, call a meeting and ask each person how they think the household could operate more smoothly. Ask each person to talk about his or her daily schedule and goals, and what he or she needs from the rest of the group for things to operate more smoothly.

- After you have done your assessment, put together a plan for how you are going to streamline your life. Include in it activities that you are going to stop performing because they don't add value, and relationships that are keeping you from being the person you want to be—relationships that are eating up your time and energy and adding no value.

- If you have a family or live with a group of people, put together a plan for how the household can run more smoothly based on the input they gave you earlier. Ask them to give you their input and how they would like it changed. Try to come to agreement. Ask each person to make a commitment to doing something differently.

- Keep reassessing and refining your own life systems and processes and encourage your family or group to do the same.

CHAPTER Summary

A company's work processes have a dramatic impact on its ability to fulfill its mission. When they are cumbersome and ineffective, they result in lost time and productivity and low morale among the people who are using them. To avoid the silo syndrome, where each area or department works independently of every other area, appoint a champion of the total work process so that it works for everyone. Work processes should be designed around customer needs and should empower the people in the organization to meet the customer's needs as efficiently as possible.

Before making a change in work processes, the current system should be studied thoroughly, and input should be gathered from the people who use the processes. As work processes are refined, careful attention should be given to ensuring that roles, responsibilities, and authority levels are appropriately and clearly defined. The people who use the processes should be involved in the refining and should take ownership of them. The work processes should be applied with flexibility and should be constantly monitored as a way of anticipating problems and obstacles before they occur.

Clue #5

Effective *work processes* are the key to quality, high performance, and efficiency. When the people of the organization help to create processes that work, they are empowered to meet the objectives of the organization and fulfill the mission.

CHAPTER 6

Clue In to Your Brand

THE KEY TO MARKETING SUCCESS

Can you describe your product or service and why it is different in four words or less? Is everyone in your company crystal clear about what the product is about? And do you have a well-defined process for communicating your uniqueness to customers and for holding everyone in the company accountable for staying true to and living up to what makes your product unique? If you answered no to one or more of the questions above, you probably haven't branded your product in the mind of the consumer.

Today, everyone is talking about branding, a business buzzword that appeared on the scene in the late 1990s. Like most business buzzwords, branding is not a new idea. It's just a fancy word for an idea that has been around a long time. It usually describes what companies should have been doing all along. Branding is the process of managing what you want your product or service to be in the mind of the consumer.

Branding actually extends beyond those functions formally identified as marketing. Everything a company does sends a message and is a form of marketing: everything from the written correspondence sent to the customer, to the greeting a caller receives when he or she calls the company, to the product or service itself. Managing those messages is no small task.

Branding is particularly important today, because the marketplace is overcrowded, and there's too much information about too many products—consumers are experiencing information overload. Proclaiming the virtues of your product or service through advertising alone will never build a brand, no matter how wonderful your product is or how creative your advertising. Everyone is saying the same thing and most consumers aren't listening.

The way consumers buy has also changed. Today, they buy more by brand than they do by recommendation of a salesperson. Branding actually presells the product or service for you. A successful branding program creates the perception in the mind of the consumer that the product or service is better than any other—that it is different and unique. It uses a multitude of means to create that perception.

In a tightened economy, companies cannot afford to waste marketing dollars. They must create powerful synergies among the various marketing disciplines so that the product or service is distinguished from the pack. The consumer must be able to hear the message above the din of promotional hoopla and perceive the product or service the way the company wants it to be. Nickelodeon President Herb Scannell, the *Blue's Clues* creators, and Nick Jr. set out to brand the television show long before branding became a buzzword.

A BRAND WITHIN A BRAND

Before *Blue's Clues* came along, Nick Jr., Nickelodeon's preschool programming block from 9 AM to 2 PM each weekday, had yet to become a brand. Designed to superserve two- to five-year-olds, just like Nickelodeon superserves older kids, Nick Jr. had established its Play to Learn philosophy as a result of exhaustive research with parents and preschoolers and the summit meeting of educators, child development experts, toy inventors, and others. The people at Nick Jr. knew what they wanted it to be—the gold standard for preschool television programming—but it had yet to become that in the minds of the consumer. *Blue's Clues* would change all that by articulating everything Nick Jr. wanted to represent.

Today, Nick Jr. is a very strong brand with an impressive line-up of programs for preschoolers: *Blue's Clues, Little Bill, Dora the Explorer,* and *Oswald,* to name a few. It has in fact become the gold standard for preschool children's television. Few people knew in the beginning, however, that *Blue's Clues* would become a brand unto its own. Not all preschool children's television shows become a brand, but this one was destined from the beginning.

FIRST ON THE SCENE

One of the best ways to brand your product or service is to be the first. Domino's was the first home-delivery pizza chain, CNN was the first cable news network, Jell-O was the first gelatin dessert. Being first automatically positions you as the leader and no one can take that away. When you create a new category of an existing product, you have virtually no competition in the beginning. It won't stay that way for long, however; nor do you want it to. Competition is good, because it helps to promote the new category.

Blue's Clues was by no means the first preschool children's television show, but it was the first to be totally interactive. It created a new category of children's television programming. Because of the interactivity, it had greater educational value than most children's television shows, which made parents look differently at preschool television programming.

When *Blue's Clues* first came on the scene, there was nothing else like it. Thanks to the success of *Blue's Clues,* the preschool children's landscape is very different. For one, a host of other shows are now interactive. Further proof of the fact that *Blue's Clues* has changed the face of preschool children's television is a study conducted by Dan Anderson, which showed that preschoolers actually watch television differently today. Since *Blue's Clues,* they are much more prone to interact with the show, regardless of whether the show invites their interaction. It's more proof of what the creators and Nick Jr. knew from the beginning: children come to television with an active mind.

PLANTING THE FLAG

From the beginning, the creators did everything they could to let it be known they were different. They wanted to "own" the color blue, so practically everything they did was in the color blue. They wanted every preschooler in America to associate the color blue, especially the blue paw print, with *Blue's Clues.* Before the show was even in production, every piece of correspondence they sent within and outside the company bore a blue paw print.

Whenever they referred to the show, they always called it a *phenomenon,* a *breakthrough television show.* They tried to be breakthrough in everything they did, from the look and design of the show, to the marketing and advertising, to the way they aired episodes. For example, the multiple viewing strategy, which aired each episode five consecutive days a week, was totally new. The multiple viewing strategy made perfect sense, because children learn from repetition and they like to watch things over and over. People, however, still had to be educated on why it was good for kids. The creators and Nick Jr. never missed an opportunity to talk about why the show was different.

Blue's Clues created a whole new world for preschoolers and a whole new lexicon: words such as Handy Dandy Notebook and the Thinking Chair. They created songs around everyday events, songs that kids would sing when they weren't watching the show. *Blue's Clues,* for example, has received scores of letters and e-mails from parents saying how the family sings the Mail Song every time the mail comes.

The use of preschooler voice-overs during the show was also new and different. It is one of the many techniques the show uses to invite the kids at home to interact. There are countless other examples of how the show is different, but the point is this: They took some big risks that paid off. They had no guarantees that they would work, and it took a lot of courage to go against conventional thinking. The risks they took were the foundation for creating the brand, because it set them apart and gave them something to talk about.

EVERY BRAND NEEDS A CHAMPION

As you can probably tell by now, the *Blue's Clues* success story is just as much about people and relationships as it is about product and events. One of the people most responsible for turning *Blue's Clues* into a brand was Ruth Sarlin, a seasoned marketing professional who was Nickelodeon's director of Nick Jr. marketing at the time of the *Blue's Clues* creation.

Ruth tells the story of the first time she saw the tape of preschoolers watching the pilot: "I knew we were making children's television history when I saw how the kids responded to the pilot," she said. "They were actually talking to the television . . . some were walking around it as though they wanted to get in it. There wasn't a silent, still child in the room and their excitement kept growing. The more excited they got, the more excited I got.

I knew this was something I could brand—all I had to do was the work."

Ruth saw instantly what the creators had achieved and from that point forward she made it her personal challenge to see that the world knew about this breakthrough children's television show. She would not rest until *Blue's Clues* was a household word. Her mission became the *Blue's Clues* mission.

The task ahead of her was enormous; she would have to get the full support of Nickelodeon's top management and the support of virtually every department within the company. Over the years, Nickelodeon had had an impressive string of hit television shows for older kids, but never one for preschoolers. Ruth was so convinced of the show's value and potential that she asked the company to support it in a big way. If it didn't work, her professional reputation would be at stake.

Turning a product into a brand usually requires vision and a tremendous amount of salesmanship, determination, and coordination across departmental lines. Many excellent products fail because they have no champion who is willing to take risks, fight for the vision, and persevere through all of the external and internal obstacles that must be overcome if a product is to become a brand.

LAUNCHING THE SHOW

Ruth wanted to do something bold to get people to watch the premiere of *Blue's Clues*—to introduce parents and preschoolers to this innovative new show. A rule breaker, just like the *Blue's Clues* creators, she worked with the advertising agency Kidvertisers to create a print ad with attitude—attitude that some thought was just a bit too edgy for a preschool children's television show. The entire ad was black with the exception of the picture of the

The ad for the *Blue's Clues* premiere. Its black background was bold and edgy for a preschool children's television show—just like the show itself.

costar, Blue. The copy read, "Finally, a preschool TV show with a clue." The ad was to capture the energy and spirit of the show. It was intended to be bold and brave just like the show.

Black was not a color associated with preschoolers, and to some, the copy could have appeared arrogant, but the ad was all about getting attention, making a very large claim and then living up to it. In Ruth's mind, it wasn't arrogance, it was fact. She knew if she could get parents to watch the show with their preschoolers, they would understand how unique and different the show was—particularly, how educational it was. They would see how much their children enjoyed and responded to the interaction the show invited.

The ad ran in all of the major parenting magazines and some general interest publications such as *TV Guide*. From the beginning, they wanted to plant the ideas *interactive* and *educational* in the minds of parents. If BMW was the ultimate driving machine in the minds of consumers, they wanted *Blue's Clues* to be the ultimate educational show for preschoolers. The primary technique the creators used to educate kids through the show was interaction, so before the show even aired they wanted to give parents and kids an experience of interaction.

The ad was actually an insert bound into magazines—almost a small magazine within a magazine. When you opened it up, it replicated the *Blue's Clues* interactive, game-playing experience by featuring games and puzzles similar to those played on the show—games that parents could actually play with their preschoolers.

To promote the educational value of *Blue's Clues,* they promoted the show to early childhood educators and day-care providers. Ruth and her team designed and sent more than 50,000 interactive kits to educators across the country and the response was overwhelming. The kit included a video of the first episode with an introductory message from Angela Santomero explaining the educational principles behind the show, a large poster with games and puzzles the teacher could play with the kids, as well as something to send home with the kids—a door knob hanger that read, "Knock, Knock, Blue's There." The educational value of the show was, in effect, communicated to parents by the educators.

From *Blue's Clues* research and the response from the teachers, they learned that teachers of preschoolers are starved for resources and ideas for educating and entertaining kids. After the initial mailing, the request for more kits was something Ruth, Nick Jr., and the creators had not expected. They had definitely reached their target audience, preschool teachers, and indirectly were able to reach parents with the news of the *Blue's Clues* premiere.

The launch campaign, which also consisted of extensive on-air promotion as well as a massive press campaign conducted by Nickelodeon's publicity department, did the job. The *Blue's Clues* premiere garnered the highest premiere rating for its demographic group in Nickelodeon history, and surpassed premiere ratings of *Sesame Street* and *Barney and Friends* as well.

The media reviews of the premiere echoed the claims made in the advertising campaign: "Finally, a Preschool TV Show with a Clue." New York *Daily News* columnist Ken Chenko said of the premiere, "Among the wealth of new preschool shows, one of the most innovative and most interactive looks to be Nickelodeon's *Blue's Clues.* The show has all the earmarks or say "paw prints" of being the cutting edge educational show for the going interactive preschool set."

Again, when parents thought of *educational* and *interactive* in relation to preschool television programming, the Nick Jr. team wanted them to think *Blue's Clues.* After the premiere all the signs were there. The foundation was set for *Blue's Clues* to become a phenomenon.

I guess I have always been a bit of a maverick. Growing up I broke the rules on a fairly regular basis, particularly when I wanted or needed to do something that was important to me. I was never spiteful or malicious—it's just what I did to get what I wanted.

Who knows what influences in our early lives shape the person we become? In many ways I had a very ordinary upbringing but my role models, my parents, were anything but ordinary—they were survivors of the Holocaust. Growing up I was particularly inspired and fascinated by my father who took enormous risks and overcame insurmountable odds just to survive. The lengths he went to and the rules he broke just to get his family to this country are beyond imagine. He was a man of integrity but he was unstoppable in his quest to survive and create a new life in a free country—something today I appreciate all the more since September 11.

Perhaps the most important thing I learned from my father is the importance of pressing on when you care deeply about something. Although my struggles pale compared to his, the example he set for me—to courageously "fight the good fight" and never settle—has influenced every aspect of my life. When I first saw the Blue's Clues *pilot, I knew immediately it was something I could care deeply about and would be willing to fight for. The creators had given birth to this ingenious show and I was fortunate enough to be one of the midwives that would help bring it into the world. It was a hard labor, but I enjoyed every minute of it.*

Ruth Sarlin

FROM HIT TO PHENOMENON

After the launch on September 9, 1996, *Blue's Clues* ratings continued to soar. Nickelodeon and *Blue's Clues* offices were flooded with letters and e-mails from parents and educators applauding and praising the show. It was obviously filling a void. After the show had been on the air for a while, many parents wanted to know where the products were. Countless parents bemoaned the fact that they were having to make their own Blue stuffed animals, green striped shirts, etc.

An article by reporter Laurie Miflin in the *New York Times* Arts section (March 1998) proclaimed in big, bold headlines: "Move Over Big Bird . . . A New Blue Dog is in Town." Other headlines echoed the same: "Oh, Hue Kid: *Blue's* Beats the Purple Guy" *(Dallas Morning News)*. *Blue's Clues* was beating its competition in the ratings and getting lots of attention in the press, but there was more to be done. It was a superhit television show, but that was it. In order to elevate it to true phenomenon status, in order for it to become a brand, something big would have to happen.

Here's where Nickelodeon and *Blue's Clues* succeeded where many companies fail. In many companies, marketing strategies fail to turn a product into a brand because the various functions involved in the marketing process—advertising, publicity, sales promotion, public affairs, and product development to name a few—fail to work together. All too often, they are at odds with one another, vying for control of the process, fighting for a bigger piece of the budget, trying to outshine one another.

They often don't value what the other functions bring to the marketing mix. Advertising and publicity are a perfect example. Advertising executives often look down their noses at public relations professionals and vice versa. Consequently, there is little cooperation and support. In order for a product or service to become a brand, the various marketing functions must work together in a seamless, cohesive manner so that the effort of one function supports and enhances the efforts of the others—so that the product or service, in the mind of the consumer, is what the company wants it to be. Nickelodeon and *Blue's Clues* were successful in creating amazing marketing synergies, which is one of the primary reasons *Blue's Clues* is a brand today, but it wasn't easy.

Nickelodeon had never had a superhit television show for preschoolers like *Blue's Clues*. The potential was enormous, but mining that potential would require a marketing campaign that was every bit as breakthrough as the show. How to make noise— how to get the world to stop and pay attention in a big way—that was the challenge. After the show became a hit, you couldn't just tell people to watch it; they were already doing that. You had to get people talking about it, and that required press, and lots of it. Press is the lifeblood of any television show. Nickelodeon has one of the best publicity departments around, but they had to have something to talk about.

Ruth knew she could not rest until she could ride down the escalator of the Viacom Building, where Nickelodeon is head-quartered, walk out onto Times Square, and be certain that if she asked any passerby if he or she had heard of *Blue's Clues,* the answer would be "yes." When that happened, she would know she had done her job. Ruth got the feedback she was seeking about two years into the life of *Blue's Clues* in a little different fashion— when she checked into a hotel and the woman working the reception desk handed her a message with *Blue's Clues* written on it. The hotel receptionist commented, "Oh, my gosh. Are you from *Blue's Clues?* That's all my nephew talks about." It wasn't a mother, but a more distant relative—even more proof that *Blue's Clues* was on its way.

To move *Blue's Clues* to the next level, Ruth presented the idea of doing a prime-time special. What better way to make a preschool show stand out than by putting a single episode in prime time? It wasn't going to be an easy sell, because Nickelodeon had never aired a preschool show in prime time. One of the things that's interesting about Nickelodeon is that an idea doesn't get implemented because of rank or title. It gets implemented because it is good. If someone in the company is passionate about something and that passion is stronger than the boss's reservations, and the person is convincing, that person gets his or her way. Ruth got her way.

She had the time slot, but what could they do that would be worthy of it? It had to be more than a usual episode. It had to be something Nickelodeon could build an elaborate campaign around. Ruth asked herself, "What is the biggest event in the life of a preschooler?" A birthday, of course. *Blue's Big Birthday Party*—that was it! The creators and Nick Jr. loved the idea and within 48 hours, Angela Santomero had written the script for the prime-time special episode, which would celebrate Blue's birthday and teach problem-solving skills. What was the problem or puzzle to be solved by Steve and the animated characters? What Blue wanted for her birthday.

The idea was there, but the biggest challenge lay ahead—how to get everyone in the company behind the promotion—how to create the synergy that would put *Blue's Clues* over the top. Nickelodeon is an amazing promotional machine—it has powerful arms and legs. In order to take advantage of Nickelodeon's promotional capability, Ruth knew she would have to build a bandwagon everyone would want to get on. She introduced the idea of creating a tent pole event that everyone could rally around, but first she would have to sell the idea, person by person, department by department. She would have to use her influence as never before.

One by one, they got on board. The promotions marketing department delivered two big-name sponsors—Mott's and Subway, both of which developed extensive promotional campaigns around the prime-time special. Nickelodeon and Nick Jr. were especially discriminating in who they enlisted as sponsors; they wanted only sponsors whose products were healthy for kids.

Mott's conducted a consumer promotion in food stores nation-wide—they changed the outside labeling of juice bottles to blue and topped them with blue bottle caps with a blue paw print on the inside. The *Blue's Clues* apple juice bottle even appeared in an episode of *Friends,* which made *Blue's Clues* and Mott's happy. Mott's also changed its applesauce for the first time in the product's history. They created—you guessed it—blue applesauce. (Remember, the *Blue's Clues* creators wanted to own the color blue.)

Subway conducted what was their most successful kids' promotion ever. The *Blue's Clues* Kid's Pack, featuring a meal and figures of all the *Blue's Clues* characters donned in birthday hats, were offered at all 12,300 Subway locations nationwide. The packs were in such demand that they sold out in a couple of days. The *Blue's Clues* Subway promotion was so successful in bringing people into the stores and moving product that they signed up for four more promotions after *Blue's Big Birthday.*

To get the attention of parents, *Blue's Clues* created the *Blue's Big Birthday Party* Sweepstakes, which viewers could enter by sending a birthday card to Blue. Blue was inundated with birthday greetings from preschoolers. The winner received a customized *Blue's Clues* birthday party with a special appearance by Steve and a $10,000 college scholarship. To encourage parents to watch the special with their kids, Rosie O'Donnell and Gloria Estefan made guest appearances on the special and wished Blue a happy birthday. There also was an extensive on-air campaign featuring a host of other celebrities wishing Blue a happy birthday.

Before the airing of the first prime-time special, *Blue's Clues* had virtually no consumer products. The Nickelodeon consumer products division jumped on the bandwagon by launching a line of upscale consumer products at the FAO Schwarz flagship store in New York. A few days after the special, which aired June 14, 1998, the store held a giant birthday party, which was attended by more than 7,000 people—in the rain! It was the most successful product launch event in the 136-year history of FAO Schwarz.

Virtually all of Nickelodeon's other ancillary businesses participated as well—everyone from the online area, whose visits increased by 44 percent, to publishing, which increased Simon & Schuster book orders from 1,500 units per title to 10,000 units per title. The tent pole event and bandwagon that delivered it accomplished its objective—it was a major turning point for the show, a true Blue phenomenon. The prime-time special received a 6.3 national rating (2.5 million people). The special outperformed ABC's *Wonderful World of Disney* (4.5 rating), the NBA championship series on NBC featuring Magic Johnson (4.2 rating), *The Simpsons* on Fox (2.9 rating), and *Touched by an Angel* on CBS (1.3 rating).

Thanks to Nickelodeon's publicity department, the press coverage was massive. Here's a small sampling of the press reviews:

- "A shining treasure in the cluttered landscape of children's television"—*New York Times*

- "Puppy love at first sight"—*People* magazine

- "The hottest preschool show since *Sesame Street*—*TV Guide*

- ". . . [T]he hottest kids' show on TV right now is *Blue's Clues* . . . The reason for *Blue's Clues* success is simple: It's one of the most engaging and imaginative series for any age group."—*Entertainment Weekly*

A NEW MODEL FOR NICKELODEON

The tent pole event strategy was so successful that a new model was created for promoting Nickelodeon's key shows, the model they still use today. Nickelodeon had always been a company where people collaborated and worked as a team, but the tent pole idea gave them something to rally around. It allowed each area to maximize its effectiveness by being part of a big event that was supported by everyone and that helped accomplish the goals of the departments which participated. Figure 6.1 shows a model that describes the various functions at Nickelodeon that work together to turn shows that have the potential into a franchise.

USING PUBLICITY TO FURTHER BUILD THE BRAND

One of the mistakes many companies make is trying to build a brand by pouring millions of dollars into advertising—a strategy that usually doesn't work. Publicity is far more powerful and much less expensive. In fact, it's virtually impossible to build a brand if it can't generate favorable publicity in the media. Publicity is generally more powerful because it has more credibility. What others say about your product or service is far more believable than what you pay your advertising agency to say.

After *Blue's Big Birthday Party*, the creators and Nickelodeon knew they had to keep working at the press. They couldn't let the wave that was building subside. Nickelodeon's publicity department put together a plan for a media blitz. Where could you go to get the best press with parents? And, who was one of the biggest kid advocates around? None other than Rosie O'Donnell. Making her first live appearance on television, Blue appeared on the *Rosie O'Donnell Show* along with Steve. They didn't just make a short appearance; the entire show was devoted to *Blue's Clues*. Rosie and the audience played *Blue's Clues* on the show. Throughout the show, paw prints kept showing up in places like band leader John McDaniel's shoulder and on Rosie's desk. Each member of the studio audience received a toy and a Blue stuffed animal. Blue and Steve's appearance on Rosie seemed to set *Blue's Clues* on an even faster track to superstardom.

FIGURE 6.1 *Brand Franchise Model*

Not long after the *Rosie O'Donnell Show* appearance, *Blue's Clues* appeared on the October 31, 1998, cover of *TV Guide*. The two-page spread inside talked about the fact that *Blue's Clues* had become a true cultural phenomenon. It went on to say: "*Blue's Clues* is one of those rare instances when conventional television is both creative and educational without sacrificing entertainment value. It savvily combines high-tech and low-tech, intensive research and gut instinct, fun and challenge."

The publicity department looked for every opportunity it could to keep *Blue's Clues* in the eye of the media. The creators did numerous interviews. Reporters accompanied *Blue's Clues* researchers as they tested episodes on preschoolers before final production. The reporters got to see firsthand how crazy kids are about the show and especially why they respond the way they do. Steve appeared on the *Today* show and *Live with Regis and Kathie Lee,* and others. *Blue's Clues* was hot and getting hotter.

FROM PHENOMENON TO ICON

Angela Santomero was sitting on the set of the *Today* show, about to be interviewed by Maria Shriver. She had been coached by Nickelodeon President Herb Scannell to take a light approach to the interview. A true visionary, Angela can sometimes be intense and serious. The subject was not funny, but it was interesting: rumors were flying over the Internet and everywhere that Steve was dead. The Nickelodeon and *Blue's Clues* offices were inundated with calls from concerned parents and the press, including the Associated Press and the *New York Times.*

Angela cares deeply about *Blue's Clues* and the impact it has on little children but when Maria Shriver asked the question in a serious, somber tone, "What was your first reaction when you learned of the rumor that Steve was dead?" Angela replied, "I was excited." Maria looked at her in disbelief, as if to say, "How could you say such a thing?"

The point was this: Angela and the *Blue's Clues* creators had gone to great lengths to inform and instruct parents on how to deal with the issue and talk to their preschoolers if they were upset. But the fact remained that when people start making up and circulating rumors about the star of a show, you know you have become a cultural phenomenon.

There were other signs that *Blue's Clues* had become a phenomenon. "Foxtrot," a comic strip for parents, made *Blue's Clues* the focus of a whole week of strips. *Blue's Clues* was a question on

Jeopardy! and the topic of a joke on *Saturday Night Live*. Rosie O'Donnell frequently gave away *Blue's Clues* products on her show. Interestingly, after one summer hiatus, she did a series of promos for her new season and one of the promos featured *Blue's Clues* almost exclusively.

Blue was also featured with a milk moustache in the "Got Milk?" ad campaign. There was one ad for parents and one for kids (chocolate milk, of course, for kids). The ad ran in parenting magazines across the country. It was a huge campaign. The National Fluid Milk Processor Promotion Board even sponsored big chocolate milk parties at day-care centers and nursery schools.

When *Blue's Clues* introduced its first direct-to-video movie, *Blue's Clues* did a "blue-carpet" premiere at Paramount Studios, where they turned the grounds into a playground for kids. The premiere, which was attended by stars such as Jodi Foster, Lisa Kudrow, and Teri Hatcher, and their children, proved to be a huge media event as well.

STAYING TRUE TO THE BRAND

When a product begins to explode like *Blue's Clues* did, more and more people get involved and the activity around the product or brand begins to escalate. What made the product so famous, what makes it so unique in the minds of the public, can be easily lost. Before you know it, the brand is weakened. It's like the secret game in which one person tells the person next to him or her a secret and then it is passed around the circle. By the time it gets to the last person in the circle, the secret hardly resembles the original secret.

When the television show started to take off and a host of ancillary businesses became involved—businesses run by various departments within Nickelodeon—the creators were vigilant about making sure everyone stayed true to the brand. Products included

Being in a Got Milk? ad is a sure sign of celebrity status. Blue helped the National Fluid Milk Processor Promotion Board promote chocolate milk in daycare centers and nursery schools nationwide.

books, videos, CD-ROMs, soft toys, hard toys, games, arts and craft toys, party supplies, food items, online products, and *Nick Jr.* magazine. Initially the creators were heavily involved in *Blue's Clues* decisions made by the ancillary business, even though they had no direct authority over them. It was soon clear though that it was impossible for the creators to maintain that level of involvement—especially when you consider that at any one point in time, more than 10,000 *Blue's Clues* products are on the market.

Somehow the creators needed to find a way to make sure everyone associated with *Blue's Clues* understood what the show was about—not just from a content standpoint but in terms of its unique attributes and what makes it so educational and good for kids. The last thing they wanted was to be another logo-slapping show. Since they had no direct authority over consumer products, the creators had to use their influence to ensure that every product was as breakthrough and educational as the show.

The *Blue's Clues* creators and some of the people in Nickelodeon's ancillary businesses tell some interesting stories about battles, if you will, waged to determine which suggested products were true to the brand. The creators needed a systematic way of conveying the *Blue's Clues* standard. Their answer to the dilemma was a program called *Blue's Clues* 101. Accompanying the program is an in-depth book that goes into great detail about the show and its unique attributes—the attributes they encourage each ancillary business to incorporate into their product as much as possible.

Some media are better able to incorporate the attributes than others, but everyone is challenged to do their best and to always think "breakthrough." The program and book provides countless good examples of products that properly reflect the brand and poor examples that do not. Anyone who works on *Blue's Clues* or any of the ancillary businesses, including outside business partners, is given the *Blue's Clues* 101 orientation. You could say the *Blue's Clues* 101 book is their "bible" for making sure everyone walks the straight and narrow and stays true to the brand.

The success of *Blue's Clues* consumer products is the story of a successful partnership that didn't happen overnight. It was a learning experience for both. The creators had to learn to trust and respect the ancillary businesses for knowing their business, and the ancillary businesses had to trust and respect the creators of *Blue's Clues* for understanding child development and what's appropriate for them, as well as understanding the attributes of the show that are quite sophisticated and not always apparent to the untrained eye.

Blue's Clues 101 is a wonderful example of how discipline is freeing. Because the ancillary businesses have very clear guidelines to work from, it frees them to be truly creative in a way that is true to the brand. *Blue's Clues* is a show with a tremendous amount of depth and substance. *Blue's Clues* 101 helps to ensure that all *Blue's Clues* products have similar depth and substance.

The creators, of course, are still involved. They meet regularly with all ancillary businesses. Angela gives feedback and guidance in terms of the product content; Traci Paige Johnson gives feedback and guidance on the design and look; and Alice Wilder is involved in research and content development. Just like episodes of the show, every product is heavily tested before it goes to market.

Here are some of the attributes covered in *Blue's Clues* 101, which ancillary business are asked to incorporate into their products:

- The show is **educational**—products should be educational.

- The show is **breakthrough**—products should be breakthrough.

- The show is **multilayered** so that it is challenging for all ages within the two- to five-year-old age range—products should be multilayered.

- Each episode **tells a story**—products should be based on a story.

- Each episode centers on a preschool **theme** such as snack time, bath time, growing, etc.—products should be theme-based.

- *Blue's Clues* is **organic** (natural) in design and in the way the story unfolds—products should have tactile features and should appear naturally as they do in real life.

- The show incorporates **game playing** and interactivity—products should be interactive and include games.

- The show allows kids to **go back** and learn something new again and again—products should allow kids to go back again and again and learn something.

- The show is **simple** and uncluttered—products should be simple as well.

- Everything in the show is developmentally **preschool appropriate**—products should be preschool appropriate.

Here are some examples of *Blue's Clues* products that are truly breakthrough—products that incorporate as many of the above attributes as possible and thereby reinforce the brand:

- The Oral-B Blue toothbrush has an ergonomic handle for preschoolers. When the toothpaste comes out of the tube, it comes out in the shape of paw prints. On the back of the toothbrush box are all kinds of games with clues. There are peel-offs on the box that kids can remove and make things with.

- Instead of selling modeling clay in round containers like the manufacturers of Play-Doh, they renamed it Play Clay

Oral-B *Blue's Clues* toothpaste squeezes out in the shape of paw prints.

Colorforms Big Easy Game can be played on two levels of difficulty.

Play Clay comes in Shovel and Pail, two characters in the show.

Mott's blue applesauce and
Kraft's Macaroni and Cheese
blue pasta in the shape
of paw prints.

The *Blue's Clues*
Hooded Towel isn't
just a bath towel–kids
become Blue, complete
with floppy ears.

Blue's Clues shoes
have "kissing fish,"
so kids can put shoes
on themselves!

and sell it in Shovel and Pail, two of the characters in the show. The clay is specially treated so that it doesn't crack and fade when it is dry like other types of clay.

- The *Blue's Clues* Big Easy Game tells a story and is multilayered. Instead of the goal being to go from start to finish, as in Candy Land and Chutes and Ladders, the game is built around a story that serves as a reason or motivation to go from start to finish. The game can be played on two different levels, depending on the age, so there are two sets of instructions.

- *Blue's Clues* apparel is designed to empower kids just like the show tries to empower them. Apparel features like bigger buttons, larger neck holes, and color matching encourage kids to dress themselves. They researched in advance with parents to determine what they wanted in apparel.

- All *Blue's Clues* shoes have "kissing fish" on the inside of the heel. When the kids have the shoes aligned so that the fish are kissing, they know they have them lined up for the right feet. If you have children, you know that it's difficult to maintain a pair of socks. One of the socks is always missing, so *Blue's Clues* socks always come in threes.

- The blue-spotted bath towel isn't a bath towel with a pose of Blue slapped on it. It *is* Blue—it is hooded, with floppy ears so that the kids can be Blue.

Nickelodeon's consumer products department and the *Blue's Clues* creators constantly try to raise the bar with their products. They encourage business partners to take their products to places they have never been before. Of the 10,000 or so products they have out there at any one time, in each category, they try to have at least one breakout product. And they have succeeded.

aking over the role of live host on Blue's Clues *is an awesome experience—exciting but a bit overwhelming at the same time. What I feel must be what Charlie Sheen felt when he took over Michael J. Fox's role on the television series,* Spin City. *The audience has a love affair with the original actor— a love affair you want to honor and at the same time you have to build your own personal relationship with the audience.*

There is no question that Steve Burns has left some big shoes for me to fill. Steve had a huge challenge when he took on the role in that he had to create almost from scratch what the live-host role for Blue's Clues *would be—he was a major force in building the brand.*

My challenge is to stay true to the brand, to what makes Blue's Clues *special and unique, and at the same time, take the live-action host role to a new level. The best way I know to do that is to be myself. If I try to be Steve, I will be a very poor imitation.*

Besides, on the show I'm not supposed to be Steve—I'm Steve's little brother, Joe. Speaking of brothers, I feel very fortunate to have in my life a wonderful inspiration for my role as Joe. I have a five-year-old little sister, who is a huge fan of Blue's Clues*—and, of course, I am a huge fan of hers. She helps to bring the child out in me, something I know will serve me well in building the character of Joe.*

I feel very blessed to have the opportunity to be an important person in the life of preschoolers. It's a responsibility I take very seriously—but not too seriously. After all, I'm just a little brother—Steve's little brother who is taking over for him because he is going off to college.

Donovan Patton

PROMOTIONAL PARTNERSHIPS THAT
BUILD THE BRAND

The key to any promotional partnership, of course, is that it be a win-win for both parties. The packaged goods area was one that had never been licensed by any company for two- to five-year-olds, so there was tremendous opportunity in that category. Promotional partners are asked to think breakthrough as well. Fruit snacks, for example, were always marketed to an older age group. In 1999, Favorite Brands launched the first fruit snacks product for preschoolers with a new softer texture and smaller packets. The back of the box featured numerous games for preschoolers to play. (Disney soon followed with a line of fruit snacks for preschoolers.)

Kraft launched *Blue's Clues* Macaroni and Cheese in the year 2000. The pasta was blue and in the shape of a paw print. The people at Kraft spent nine months developing the right shade of blue that would not turn the cheese green.

The Mott's promotion, which began with the *Blue's Big Birthday* prime-time special, was significant because it was the first time Mott's had ever done a promotion to kids, and it was the first time they had ever partnered with an entertainment company. The promotion was originally designed to be a five-month relationship, what they call in the trade a "quick in and out" product, but when Mott's saw how successful it was, they signed on for the long term.

It was a huge risk for Mott's in the beginning, because *Blue's Clues* was just beginning to really take off. When they saw how it moved product and how it enabled them to gain access to outlets they had not be able to gain entrance to before—outlets such as Wal-Mart—they signed on to be a permanent licensee. Mott's even received the EMMA (Entertainment Marketing Award) from *Promo* magazine in 1999 for jump-starting the sleepy applesauce category with *Blue's Clues* applesauce, new blue-colored applesauce big kids love as well as little kids because of its "cool" factor.

In 2000, Ford Motor Company entered into a three-year strategic alliance with *Blue's Clues*. Ford has a huge program for promoting automobile safety for kids. Blue is the official spokespuppy for Ford's Windstar Minivan Safety Program, which educates parents and kids about car safety. Blue is used in many of their promotional materials and there is even a Web site for the safety program. Ford is also the sponsor of the *Blue's Clues* live theatrical show.

OTHER ANCILLARY BUSINESSES THAT PROMOTE THE BRAND

Here are some of *Blue's Clues* other ancillary businesses run by Nickelodeon and how they are breakthrough—how they reinforce the brand.

Publishing

CD-ROMs are a natural extension of the show because of the interactive feature of both the show and CD-ROMs. The producers actually film part of the CD-ROMs on the *Blue's Clues* set so that they are true to the television show. Nickelodeon and *Blue's Clues* have released six *Blue's Clues* CD-ROMs, which have won numerous awards similar to the Emmy's for television.

In the book category, *Blue's Clues* has been one of the top book franchises for preschoolers for the last four years. Translating the attributes of the show to books is quite challenging, but they do it. For example, one way they try to make it interactive is by drawing in the caregiver who is reading the story. The caregiver is asked to physically do something as he or she reads the story.

Blue's Clues books are designed to reinforce the learning on the show. In *Blue's Lost Backpack,* for example, a method for finding lost objects, which was introduced on an episode, is reinforced. In the episode and in the book, Steve and Blue, "go, back, go back, go back, go back to where we were." This gives preschoolers a strategy and life skill for dealing with situations in which they have lost something.

Online Content

Nick Jr. uses its Web site, Nick Jr.Com, to introduce preschoolers to their first Internet experience. It's an ideal medium for extending the learning on the television show because it allows kids to be even more interactive than they are with the show. Nick Jr.Com, the premier Web site for kids two to six years of age, provides Web sites for all Nick Jr. shows. On the *Blue's Clues* site, there are more than 45 games, which are extensions of episodes. It also includes interactive stories, an art area, e-cards, coloring pages, recipes kids can make with their parents, party ideas, and party decorations, to name a few. There are over 50 printables that can be printed off the computer.

The *Blue's Clues* Web site also has a host of activities for parents and preschoolers to do together as a way of furthering parental involvement. Computers will be very much a part of preschoolers future life and education, so Nick Jr.Com gives them as many different kinds of online experiences as possible. For example, when Steve, the first host, left the show to "go off to college," the kids were encouraged to send him an e-mail, to which he responded.

Nick Jr. Magazine

Nick Jr. magazine, which has a circulation of 800,000, does something no other parenting magazine does—it speaks to kids and parents together. There's a section for parents, a section with games and activities strictly for kids, and a section that provides a host of games and activities kids and parents can do together.

The part of the magazine devoted to *Blue's Clues* is also an extension of the show. It contains many of the attributes of the show. It's educational, multilayered, interactive, theme-based, and organic.

A CONSUMER PRODUCT SUCCESS STORY

Since most children's television shows have about a three-year life, introducing consumer products can be risky. Nickelodeon and Nick Jr. never introduce products until two things happen: they know the show is a hit, and parents and kids are asking for products. It wasn't long after the show's premiere that they knew it was a hit and parents started demanding products, but the consumer products department was not about to rush to market. Once again, the consumer product marketing strategy was breakthrough—they went against convention and what the competition was doing at the time.

From the beginning, the consumer products department managed the business for the long term. They developed a strategy that would ensure long-term success—a strategy based on long-term strategic alliances with outside promotional partners and licensees, something that isn't traditional with licensees who are often in it for short-term gain. And they were very selective about who they partnered with. There were two requirements: the partner had to be the best in its category and its product had to be good for kids.

They also didn't want to oversaturate the market with *Blue's Clues* products. Instead, they introduced it slowly—first to upscale boutiques or high-end stores, then to midtier stores, and finally to mass market. They didn't want to compete just on price—they wanted to keep the product special. It was a tough decision to hold to, because another show, *Teletubbies* was releasing product like crazy. The consumer products department didn't want *Blue's Clues* to burn itself out—instead, it was treated as an evergreen property.

The strategy worked and continues to work. Today there are more than 75 *Blue's Clue's* licensees. Business partners are the best in their categories: Hallmark, Fisher-Price, Kids Headquarters, and Kraft, to name a few. Business partners love *Blue's Clues,* because it provides them with the opportunity to create breakthrough products that accomplish their own business objectives.

As Hallmark Licensing Product Manager Curt Creason says: "Hallmark is one of the top five most recognizable brands in the country, so it made sense that we would want to partner with a children's television show that also had incredible brand recognition. The values of our two companies are so similar and we both bring so much to the table, it's no surprise that the partnership has vaulted Hallmark/*Blue's Clues* products to a top-selling position in our product categories including party supplies, greeting cards, and gift wrapping. It's a total win-win for both companies."

Since *Blue's Clues* consumer products were introduced in 1998, *Blue's Clues* has sold over $3 billion in product. They've sold over one million of Steve's green striped shirt and over six million Handy Dandy Notebooks. *Blue's Clues* products have won countless Parent's Choice Awards, LIMA (Licensing Industry Manufacturers Association) awards, the Sears Innovation Award, Best Children's Educational Software Awards (BESSIES), and a host of others.

MAINTAINING THE BRAND

Maintaining a brand once it is established can be every bit as challenging as creating it. It's challenging because the world around your product is constantly changing. If you've achieved brand status, you can be sure your competition is watching you closely and taking steps to take market share away from you. If you are the keeper of the brand, you can never rest.

One of the greatest branding sins companies commit is losing focus, succumbing to the temptation to fundamentally change what made your product a brand in the first place. You have to trust your brand, which means you don't change course every time the competition does something new and different.

The creators of *Blue's Clues* and Nick Jr. believe that one of their primary jobs is navigating what's good for the brand. Sometimes the waters get tricky because what's best is not always readily apparent. When you've achieved a certain level of success, a lot of people and outside companies make some attractive offers that can be quite lucrative in the short term but that can compromise the brand in the long run.

At *Blue's Clues,* they have three basic rules for maintaining the brand:

1. Stay true to what made *Blue's Clues* a brand in the first place.

2. Consistently find ways to keep the television show fresh and new.

3. Keep *Blue's Clues* in the press by creating ongoing events that allow them to talk about why the show is unique and special.

One of the ways they keep the show in the media is through ongoing prime-time specials and tent pole events, similar to *Blue's Big Birthday.* The tent pole event strategy has been so finely tuned that today it is a vehicle for promoting very targeted business initiatives beyond the scope of the show.

One of the reasons the prime time specials and the promotional events around them succeed is because *Blue's Clues* keeps searching for the touchstones of a preschooler's life—events that are particularly significant to them. *Blue's Clues* could do all the hype in the world, but if the theme didn't resonate with the kids, it wouldn't work.

In 1999, the Nick Jr. marketing department choreographed the tent pole event surrounding the prime-time special, *Blue's Big Treasure Hunt,* which also garnered strong ratings. The multitiered promotion included a real treasure hunt in over 600 Sears stores nationwide, as well as a Treasure Hunt Sweepstakes, which sent ten families to Jamaica for a treasure hunt with Steve.

One of the most successful prime-time specials was *Blue's Big Pajama Party* in 2000. Julia Louis-Dreyfus made a guest appearance at the beginning of the show. The advertising campaign encouraged kids and their families to "tune in and snuggle up," and to come to the show in their pajamas. Nickelodeon, Nick Jr., and *Blue's Clues* executives came to work in their pajamas on the day of the special, which got some interesting press.

One of the ways the creators keep the show and the franchise fresh and new is by constantly introducing new characters. *Blue's Big News,* a prime-time special that aired October 2001, featured the birth of Cinnamon. In addition to building preschooler's problem-solving skills, the episode was designed to help preschoolers get excited about and adjust to having a new baby brother or sister. Having a new baby in the house is definitely a huge event in the life of a preschooler, which is probably one reason the ratings for this special went through the roof.

When Steve Burns announced that he was leaving the show, Nick Jr. and the creators used it as an opportunity to give the show a whole new look. The show got a new host and the host got a new shirt. A new Handy Dandy Notebook was introduced and the music was changed. After six years on the air, the show was ready for a new look and the new host, "Joe," provided a wonderful opportunity to refresh the show.

Education, interactivity, and diversity are the underpinnings of the show—they are fundamental to what makes *Blue's Clues* a brand. Nick Jr. and the creators are constantly talking to parents and educators about the educational value of the show, and they constantly look for new and different ways to extend the learning. One of the episodes that received the greatest response from educators and parents was the episode on sign language. *Blue's Clues* is a very visual show and the host, Steve, was so gestural that teaching preschoolers sign language seemed like a natural extension. Academy Award winner Marlee Matlin helped launch the sign language initiative by taping sign language segments with Steve and later appearing as a guest on the show. Ever since the initial "Signs" segment, every *Blue's Clues* episode has included sign language, which has elicited an overwhelming response from viewers, particularly from the deaf community.

CLUES FOR Turning Your Product into a Brand

Turning your product into a brand is the ultimate marketing challenge and one of the keys to achieving phenomenal business results. Here are some guidelines for making it happen:

- Clearly define what you want to be in the mind of the consumer. You should be able to express it in four words or less.

- Try to make your product a first, or create a new category within an existing product.

- Make sure your product is such that it provides you with a lot to talk about in the press.

- Make sure the product has a champion within the company who can get things done.

To: *Blue's Clues*

Subject: Thank you for being smart!!!

YEA! Watching *Blue's Clues* today was the highlight of the year in our house!! Just last week I wrote to you about seeing Steve use sign language, and asking for more . . . I'm not sure if today's show was already planned with the extra signs at the end, or not . . . but I can't tell you how WONDERFUL it felt to see Steve signing again!!

Have you ever heard a deaf child holler out with utter excitement? If not, I'm really surprised you didn't hear it all the way from Ohio this morning . . . my son saw Steve and his grandma sign "thank you" AND "smart," and he proceeded to go bonkers! He wants to know if Steve is "learning to be deaf." (I had to laugh at how he put that one!)

Thank you, thank you, thank you!!! I cannot tell you how happy this has made my son and me, as well as many other deaf children, their siblings, and their parents, I'm sure!

Kudos to your show, and God bless each and every one of you! Again, my phone is ringing off the hook! Everyone is so impressed with the effort your show is making!

Thank you again,
Kimberly Bentley

- Hold the various marketing functions accountable for working collaboratively and synergistically.

- Resist the temptation to pour big dollars into expensive advertising campaigns—publicity is the key.

- Create an ongoing series of events that allow you to keep your product in the news.

- Always, always live up to the claims you make in your advertising and promotions.

- Develop a system for communicating to everyone in the company what makes your product unique and special—hold everyone accountable for staying true to what the product was originally created to be.

- Educate outside vendors and business partners on what makes your product unique and different—hold them accountable for staying true to the brand.

CLUES FOR "Branding" Yourself in the Workplace

Branding doesn't apply just to products; it also applies to people. Branding is about preselling or predisposing people to think and act in a certain way about a product or a person. Here are some guidelines for creating a "brand" of yourself in the workplace:

- Don't be afraid to be different, but be different for a reason.

- Write down a defining statement about yourself, a statement that summarizes in one sentence what you would like people to think when they hear your name.

- Be very clear about what makes you unique or different. Communicate your uniqueness to people who can influence your career in a way that shows confidence as well as humility.

- Be authentic—the "real thing," the real you.

- Be consistent in what you believe, say, and do. Live true to your defining statement.

- Look for subtle ways to market yourself to decision makers— in ways that don't alienate other people.

- Be a team player—support other people in their ambitions and they will support you.

- Make sure your image is consistent with how you wish to be perceived—ask for feedback from trusted friends and colleagues.

- Find a good mentor who can help you grow and promote your good qualities to others.

CHAPTER Summary

If a company wants to turn a product into a brand, it must first decide what the company wants it to be in the mind of the consumer. The product should be designed so that it is a first or so that it creates a new category within an existing product. The brand should be defined in simple, powerful terms and communicated to the rest of the organization as well as outside vendors and business partners.

The marketing strategy should be designed to establish and reinforce the brand. All of the elements and disciplines involved in executing the strategy (advertising, sales promotion, public relations, etc.) must work collaboratively and synergistically in order for the product to achieve brand status in the marketplace and fulfill its potential. Continuously look for and create opportunities for talking about your product in the press.

Every brand must have a champion who can work across departmental lines to ensure that all of the activities work together to create a strong presence. Guidelines should be established for helping various disciplines in the organization stay true to the brand. Everyone in the organization should understand that everything they do either supports the brand or detracts from the brand.

Clue #6

When you are crystal clear about who and what you want to be in the mind of your customer, and you manage every detail of your business so that customers see you as being in a class of your own, you will have **branded** your product.

CHAPTER 7

Clue In to Your Leadership and Management

UNCOMMON LEADERSHIP

If you lead a company, a department, or a team, you know that being a leader is a very tough job. The work is easy; people are difficult. Getting people to work harmoniously toward a common goal is nothing short of an art.

If you worked in a company or organization for any length of time, you know the suffering people experience when they have to work under poor leadership. If people don't like or respect their boss or the management of the company, the likelihood is they won't like their jobs and they will contribute to the company only a fraction of their potential.

If you have had the good fortune to work under enlightened leadership, you know the joys that come from working for someone who creates an atmosphere where people are able to excel, grow, and produce work they are proud of—where people are able to experience the camaraderie and sense of achievement that can come only from being a part of a high-performing team. There is nothing like it.

Unfortunately, too many people in our country are unhappy in their jobs due to poor leadership. According to an article in the *New York Times,* 80 percent of all working Americans are unhappy about their careers. In a study conducted by Watson Wyatt World-wide on the issue of trust, more than half of the people surveyed said they didn't trust their executive managers.

It's surprising when you consider the fact that managers have more access to knowledge and information about management than ever before. All you have to do is look at the number of books in the bookstore on the subject. Companies spend billions of dollars each year on sophisticated training programs designed to give managers the skills they need to lead people effectively. We probably have the best-trained managers in the world. So what is the problem? The truth is this: good leadership is about much more than just having an intellectual understanding of the principles of leadership and management—as you will see in the story that follows.

STARTING AT THE TOP

The story of how the *Blue's Clues* leadership team evolved is a fascinating one, as you will see in the remainder of this chapter. We haven't focused on Nickelodeon's leadership throughout this book, but it is important to note that the *Blue's Clues* phenomenon was allowed to grow and flourish because Nickelodeon President Herb Scannell and his executive staff were willing to take a chance on a group of talented young people who were hungry for an opportunity.

As mentioned previously, one of the unique aspects of the Nickelodeon culture is that it doesn't matter if you are young or old, if you are a clerk or an executive: if you have a good, creative idea that has merit, it will get heard and executed. Nickelodeon not only took a risk on the *Blue's Clues* leadership, but they gave them a combination of support and freedom that allowed them to realize their vision and create a phenomenon. The risk has paid off handsomely for Nickelodeon.

THE SITUATION

Just imagine that you are one of six people in their 20s who have just been handed a once-in-a-lifetime career opportunity. The members of your group don't know each other very well, but you all know one thing: you are going to have to call on every ounce of talent, knowledge, and experience you have in order to meet the enormous challenge before you. As a group, you are getting ready to venture into the unknown, because no one has ever done what you are about to do. You have a clear vision and the support of a successful corporation but you have no idea how you are going to climb the mountain. And you are going to need a lot of people for the climb.

What we have just described is the situation in which the *Blue's Clues* creators and other members of the senior staff found themselves in the beginning. They had to build a production company from scratch, a company that would enable them to turn their vision into a viable business and fulfill their mission. The story of how they did it is a powerful lesson in leadership.

This book is first and foremost a book about leadership, because nothing we have covered in any of the other chapters could have been accomplished without strong leadership. Nothing much happens in any organization without leadership. What makes their story particularly interesting is that none of them had ever started a business and they had little or no management experience when they began.

THE STRUGGLES

The *Blue's Clues* story as told thus far may seem almost too good to be true. The story has in no way been inflated—they really are that good at what they do. The road to getting to where they are today, however, has been a difficult one. They are the first to admit that they have made thousands of mistakes, particularly in the areas of management and leadership. The fact that they even survived the early years is a miracle in itself.

Today, you would be hard pressed to find a stronger, more cohesive leadership team or a more solid, well-run organization. They are a model for how to create a true team-based environment where people want to come to work; where people have a strong sense of ownership and pride in what they do; and where they are able to grow and reach their potential as individuals while helping the company reach its potential. Before they could arrive at this place, they had a number of challenges and obstacles to overcome. Following are just some of them.

So Much Work, So Little Time

In the beginning, there was so much to be done that almost all of their efforts were focused on the work. In the first eight months, they had to produce ten episodes, which was a monumental task. They had a small staff with which to accomplish it, a staff that knew nothing about the show, because it had never been produced; it existed only in pilot form. At that time, people were not banging down the door to work there like they are today, so hiring good people was a challenge.

They had little time to think about the work needs of the people or how the work could best be done. Everyone was flying by the seat of their pants, trying to meet the deadlines. Before long, people started to express needs. Problems between people started to occur because there was little or no organization to the work. Everyone, including the leaders, were becoming exhausted. It was not unusual for the leaders and some of the members of the staff to work 24 hours straight.

Ego Problems

Everyone on the senior staff had a sense that the show was going to be a huge hit. They were all young and starting to build their careers, so the issue of credit—who was going to get the spotlight—was something they began to struggle with. Each was concerned about whether the leaders at Nickelodeon would be able to fully recognize their contribution to the show's success. They didn't know if the pie would be big enough for all of them.

No Clear Roles

In the beginning, everyone on the senior staff did virtually everything together. Hardly a decision was made that wasn't made by the group. It was part of their strength but it also caused problems. Because they all had little experience in what they were trying to achieve, they came to rely heavily on the wisdom of the group. Together, they were confident they could figure anything out. The problem was that no one had a clear role. No one knew what he or she was uniquely contributing to the entire process because they were doing everything together. And as they grew, they simply couldn't spend the time it took to get everybody's opinion. They had to make more decisions on their own.

Too Much Inclusivity

Not only did they include each other in almost every decision, but they included the staff in most decisions. Everyone weighed in on almost everything, regardless of whether it was their area of expertise. In the beginning, it worked well because people felt very invested; everyone felt a sense of ownership. They felt very important to the process. Before too long though, the decision-making process became cumbersome and time consuming.

HOW THEY GOT TO THE OTHER SIDE

The issues we just described, of course, were not unique to the *Blue's Clues* senior team. These are the very issues that cause most start-ups to fail. It was so difficult in the beginning that each of the members of the team confesses to wanting to abandon ship at sometime during the process. They persevered, though—they stayed in the fire and kept working at their issues. As a result, they were transformed, individually and as a team.

Through their struggles and their growth process, they were able to keep good people, many of whom are still with them today. They were able to keep people in spite of the fact that they were committing a multitude of management sins, not intentionally, but because they just didn't know at the time to do differently. Following are some of the reasons they kept people with them and transformed into the strong team and organization they are today.

A Strong Vision

From the very beginning, they had a crystal-clear vision of where they were going and what they wanted to achieve. Not only did they have a clear vision, but they were passionate about it. Every member of the team was totally committed. They believed so strongly in what they were doing and were so enthusiastic about it, that it was infectious. Their vision was the driving force behind everything they did. It provided a powerful focus for mobilizing their own energy and the energy of the people they were leading.

Leadership is about vision and being able to impart that vision to the people you are leading. They were able to keep their vision so alive in the minds and the hearts of the people they were leading that people stuck with them even though some of their work needs weren't being met. Their vision was what united them.

Willingness to Look at Themselves and Change

One of the problems with many leaders is they can't face their own weaknesses. Instead of going through the hard work of searching themselves and asking what they might be doing wrong when something fails, they pass the blame onto their people. The *Blue's Clues* senior staff went through an enormous amount of soul searching, individually and as a team. Extreme stress brings out the weaknesses in everyone's personality and they were no exception. They faced themselves, and as a result they were able to grow.

When they realized they were deficient in management skills, they became students of management. The Nickelodeon training department provided them with extensive management and leadership. They read books and constantly checked in with each other to discuss how they should handle various employee situations and problems. They were able to learn from their experiences. They made a point of learning from the negative feedback they got from employees. Instead of justifying their own actions when they were wrong, they admitted it, resolved to do better, and moved on. People respected them for that.

Good Hearts

A good heart and concern for others won't necessarily ensure your business or leadership success, but it goes a long way. Every single member of the senior team truly cares about people. They are compassionate and are able to empathize and see things from other peoples' perspectives.

From the beginning, they wanted to create a very different kind of organization from most television productions. Instead of hiring people for a season and then letting them go like most productions, they wanted to build a strong organization of people who would stay with them. Creating a nurturing, supportive work environment was always just as important to them as their own personal success and the success of the show. Because people knew they had good hearts, they stuck with them, even though they made a lot of mistakes.

A Net for Each Other

Although they had their struggles and conflicts, they always stuck together. They knew they would never succeed otherwise. They got to know one another as people and found that they really liked one another. They learned about each other and helped each other find their place on the team.

Their strong relationships with one another continues to be the foundation for their success. The staff saw how they respected and supported one another, which influenced how the staff treated one another. The respect and care with which they treated each other created a positive work environment for everyone, an environment that still exists today.

Committed to "the Baby"

They looked at the show as their "baby." It was something they had conceived and if they didn't see it through, it would die. The thought of that was what kept them hanging in there on days they wanted to quit. It's also what caused them to put their egos aside, and in doing so, they found there was plenty of spotlight for everyone. Today each of them are very secure in their role on the team.

A Few Good Rules

In the beginning, they didn't have a clearly defined leadership philosophy or management processes in place, but they did have three rules, which guided them then and which still guide the organization today. The following rules are at the heart of their current management philosophy and have played a major role in their success:

1. You must jump in and say "yes" before you say "no." One of the reasons they are so breakthrough in everything they do is because they have trained themselves to work from a clean slate, without any preconceived ideas. Ideas are their stock and trade, so they guard them fiercely. It's also a way they have of showing respect for one another, by not reacting or judging someone else's contribution too quickly.

2. Split the difference. When you get a bunch of creative people together, things can get pretty hairy. People get attached to

their own ideas and have a hard time seeing the value in the other person's viewpoint. At *Blue's Clues,* they believe that the best idea is usually a fusion of two, three, or four ideas. Whenever people get into a heated discussion, each defending their own preference or point of view, someone will say, "split the difference." It is a reminder to one another that the best ideas come when people are willing to compromise, when they don't become so attached to their own ideas that they can't see another way.

3. You must say why. No one had or has today the luxury of just saying they don't like something or that they disagree. They must always tell why. If they can't describe why they feel the way they do, the opinion has no merit. It's a rule that both managers and employees apply. Managers never, never send work back to employees or reject an idea without giving them a thorough explanation.

BLUE'S CLUES LEADERSHIP TODAY

As senior staff member Dave Palmer said, "When you are sitting in a room with a large group of employees who are unhappy with you as a manager and they are firing questions at you, you learn real fast. It's like being in a room with an 800-pound gorilla. You either learn how to manage or you don't survive." And learn they did.

Today, they have a very clear management philosophy and they have mastered the principles and fundamentals of management and leadership as well as any company around. They got there by trying a lot of things that didn't work and by learning everything they could about management. They didn't just learn about the principles and fundamentals of management, but they applied them. As mentioned in the introduction of this book,

This message appeared on the Nick Jr. Web site message board for parents:

Hi, everyone. I was so glad when I found these message boards. It's nice to know there are other adults out there as obsessed with Blue as I am. My husband thinks I am crazy and says I'm more obsessed with Blue than the kids are. I even tape the episodes if I'm going to be out. I started watching *Blue's Clues* four years ago with my 3-year-old stepdaughter, who is now 7. I have my own daughter, who is 11 months old, and we started watching Blue when she was 3 months old. I only wish I had known about all the Blue baby stuff when I decorated her room. Whenever we go shopping, we look for any tapes we don't have.

My older stepdaughters, ages 13 and 17, still ask what's going on in the shows, and lately my husband actually watched a few episodes. He's a mailman, so he always gets kids on his route singing the mail song and has to laugh.

I think it's one of the greatest shows ever. I do think they should make cool Blue's clothes for us obsessed adults. We love you Blue, Steve, and friends!

they walk the talk better than any leadership team the author has ever seen.

Their philosophy is also a product of the Nickelodeon culture. The senior staff had been given a tremendous amount of empowerment by Nickelodeon and they wanted to pass it on to their staff. Their management philosophy and practices are also a product of their common sense. They spent endless hours as a leadership team, discussing virtually every employee situation or problem of any significance that arose. They talked about bosses they had had at other companies they didn't want to be like.

Out of that dialogue emerged a common philosophy and style of management that they apply consistently across the organization. One of the reasons they have such a high level of trust with their employees, as you will see in the next chapter, is because they are congruent in what they believe in their hearts, what comes out of their mouths, and what they do. The messages they send to employees are remarkably consistent.

When they formulated the mission statement for the show in the very beginning, they were unaware that they were actually crafting what would become their management philosophy as well. The mission of the show is to empower, challenge, and build the self-esteem of preschoolers while making them laugh. That is precisely how they see their mission as leaders in terms of their staff. They work very hard at empowering their people, challenging them, building their self-esteem, and providing a fun, enjoyable work environment. More than anything else, it is the secret to their success.

Perhaps the quality each of them possesses that contributes most to their success as leaders is that they are authentic—they are real and very human. It's the quality that causes employees to walk to the end of the earth for a leader, particularly if the leader has a strong vision like they do at *Blue's Clues*. People are searching for meaning and direction in their lives, and when they find a leader who has a vision and who is genuine, they naturally want to follow them. There is so much artificiality and superficiality in the world, that when people experience the "real thing," particularly in the workplace, it is like a breath of fresh air. It is no small wonder that the employee turnover rate at *Blue's Clues* is practically zero.

FINDING THE BALANCE

Effective leadership is all about striking the right balance, which is not an easy thing to do. It was one of the major challenges the senior leadership team had to face. They had to work out the balance on countless issues. Here are just some of the ways they create a harmonious work environment that meets the goals of the business:

- They pay attention to detail but they stay focused on the overall mission of the show. At first, every detail was of monumental importance. They had to learn what was of critical importance and what was not.

- They are committed to a plan, but they are not afraid to change the plan when new information is presented. They had to learn to be incredibly flexible.

- They provide everyone with a very clear description of their roles and responsibilities, but they give people plenty of opportunities to grow beyond and outside of their jobs.

- They have very clearly defined work processes and guidelines, but within those guidelines they encourage people to be as creative as they can possibly be.

- They provide people with very clearly defined standards and guidance up front but they allow and expect them to manage themselves.

- They require people to live by the consequences of their actions but they never place blame or judgment. They know that natural consequences are a better teacher than guilt and shame.

- They place a high value on order and efficiency but they recognize that creativity and innovation usually involves chaos.

- They are consistent but flexible. When it comes to their values and principles they are unyielding, but they are willing and able to change their views and direction when the situation calls for it.

- They are honest but they try to speak the truth in ways that do not hurt other people.

- They value and strive for high performance, but they never forget that behind every job is a human being with needs that must be balanced with the needs of the job.

- When they go to work, they show up and are fully present. But when they leave work, they are fully present for the other parts of their lives. Each has a very full personal life; employees are encouraged to do the same.

WORKING WITHIN THE SYSTEM

Not only do they do an excellent job of managing the *Blue's Clues* staff, but they do a superb job of managing up and outside their organization. In many ways they are a self-contained unit. They are even headquartered in a separate building from the parent, Nickelodeon, and the division to which they report, Nick Jr. At the same time, they have to work within the Nickelodeon system. For one, they are very much involved in the work of the ancillary business operated by Nickelodeon, which is one of the reasons they have been able to create and maintain such a strong brand.

It's one thing to be able to manage the people below you but another to be able to negotiate the needs of the production with the larger organization. All of the senior staff do an excellent job of that, but no one does it better than Executive Producer Jennifer Twomey, to whom we introduced you in Chapter 5. While Nickelodeon itself is a very entrepreneurial organization and extremely supportive of *Blue's Clues,* a healthy tension must be maintained between the needs and wants of the parent and those of the production. Without that tension, one of the two, if not both, would be compromised.

All of the members of the senior staff have contact with Nickelodeon, but a big part of Jen Twomey's job is to manage the budget, communicate the needs of the production to Nickelodeon, and communicate directives from Nickelodeon back to *Blue's Clues.* She also manages the relationships with the ancillary businesses. She has an amazing ability to maintain a clear head and keep her composure in the toughest of situations—situations under which most people would crumble. When she articulates the needs of the production to other people, she does so with great conviction and assertiveness but she is respectful and mindful of the needs of others at the same time. She fights hard for what she thinks the production needs, but when the answer is given, she accepts it and even if she doesn't agree with it, she presents it to *Blue's Clues* in a positive manner. As a result, she is highly respected by both her peers and the people at Nickelodeon.

One of the marks of a leader is that he or she is able to maintain emotional control under pressure, which is something that is extremely hard to do, particularly when you are so heavily invested in something. Jen is also a voice of reason with the other members of the senior staff. When she can, she shields them from a crisis when it happens, deals with it in her own quiet way, and informs them once it is resolved.

*ome things must be innate. My mother tells me that from the time I
was little, I insisted on doing things a certain way. According to my young self,
there was a right way and a wrong way of doing things and I had to do it right.
If I ever colored outside the lines, I tore up the page and started over.*

*As I grew up, I applied that thinking to just about everything I did—that is,
until I went to work at Blue's Clues. When the other members of the senior staff
and I started the show, we had a monumental task before us and they were looking to me to lead the way. I was about to learn a major life lesson.*

*I had to immediately begin making decisions and lots of them—decisions
that at the time I wasn't sure were right or wrong. As a leader I thought I had to
have all the answers and I had never been one to show any chinks in the armor,
which meant there were times when the stress level got pretty high.*

*Sometimes being thrown into the fire is the best thing that can happen. I had
to face the thing that I was afraid of: making mistakes. I was stretching so far,
doing things I had never done so I, along with the other members of the senior
team, was making mistakes left and right. I learned that my mistakes didn't cause
the show to come crashing down around us—quite the contrary. They were the
stepping stones to the place we are today. They were my best teacher.*

*Something else happened to me along the way. When I began to relax, I
realized the people I was leading were responding to me differently. Because I
no longer had to have all the answers, I was able to engage them in the problem-
solving process. Everyone, myself included, was able to be a lot more creative,
and in their eyes I think I became more approachable.*

*Today, as a result of my experience at Blue's Clues, I feel so much freer to
take risks, to share ideas, to color outside the lines, and to stumble now and then.
In fact, some of my proudest accomplishments have come from climbing out on
the limb—from throwing out ideas that before I would have prejudged in my*

own mind and kept to myself. It's Blue's Clues's *gift to me, a gift I try to give to the people I lead and a gift I want to give to my new son, Ethan. I want him to know it's okay to make mistakes—that he doesn't have to be perfect, that he can be anything he wants to be.*

Jennifer Twomey
Executive Producer

HOW THEY APPLY THEIR MANAGEMENT PHILOSOPHY

As discussed earlier, the mission of the show applies to the *Blue's Clues* management philosophy as well. That is not to imply that they treat people like children. In fact, they manage people in such a way that they are able to be more responsible and autonomous than in most organizations. Everyone, regardless of age, needs to feel empowered and challenged and they need to feel good about themselves. And if they aren't having a good time at work, what is it all for? Here's how they do it:

Empower

One way they empower people is by continuously giving them the big picture. They let people know what is coming down the road so they can plan for it. They go to great lengths to keep the vision in front of people so they always have a framework for their decision making.

One reason people and departments are able to manage themselves so well is because their roles, responsibilities, and decision-making authorities are so clearly defined. People are very clear about standards and expectations and they have very clearly defined processes for everything they do. Their discipline frees them to be more creative because they know what is expected of them and what the guidelines are.

Each department has a very clear understanding of what every other department does, which helps them work in a collaborative fashion. The department heads have unusually strong relationships with one another, in part because the members of the senior staff have such strong relationships with each other. The result is that they have a very flexible organization, which can quickly adapt and change to whatever is put in front of them. Obstacles and issues are resolved at the department level instead of going back up to the next level, which can be very time consuming. People and departments have a feeling that they can make things happen. They don't get mired down in bureaucracy and corporate politics.

Another way they empower people is by keeping them connected to their customer. Almost everyone in the organization at some time accompanies the research department to preschools to test episodes. This way they get to see directly how the kids are responding to their work.

They also give everyone in the production information about their customer—information such as where preschoolers are developmentally, what their needs are, the speed at which they grow, and so on. For example, the short book *Mollie Is Three* is recommended reading for everyone. The story helps the reader understand what is going on in the life of a child at that age and how that child is changing. It's not unusual to see people such as the sound engineers reading *Mollie Is Three* in between takes.

Challenge

The senior staff has a philosophy that everyone in the organization should be on a career escalator, constantly growing and preparing themselves for the next position. They work to stretch people by giving them tasks just a little beyond their abilities.

The work ethic and sense of pride is so high at *Blue's Clues* that people and departments challenge each other. Because their work process is so collaborative, they are frequently exposed to each other's work so they make a strong effort to ensure that they reflect well on their own departments. Superior work is expected; it is the norm, not the exception. They get a kick out of impressing one another with their work.

Once a month they have an all-staff meeting called a "clue-in" (which is where the titles for this book's chapters originated), in which each department showcases its work. Presentations are sometimes quite elaborate, with each department engaging in friendly competition.

Whenever possible, they try to promote people from within instead of hiring from the outside. Senior staff is always watching people, looking to see who is getting "itchy"—who needs a new challenge to stay inspired. The challenge might be in the form of a special project that requires the staffer to learn something new or a new position that is a stretch for him or her. Whenever they give an assignment, they encourage people to take things as far as they can before asking for help.

Build Self-Esteem

The senior staff knows how important praise and recognition is to them so they make a point of giving as much of it as they can to their staff. Not only do they give it to their staff, but they give it to each other. The senior staff are very affirming of one another, which sets an example for the rest of the staff.

The senior staff thrives on giving people challenges, helping them grow and watching them achieve—it's one of the true secrets of their success. They frequently sit in on weekly departmental meetings where work is being presented and reviewed. They never miss an opportunity to acknowledge a person's fine work when they see it.

They have a bimonthly newsletter called the *Fortnightly,* which is not your standard company newsletter. It's printed on plain memo paper and the quote under the heading reads, "Some of the news that's fit to print, and then some other stuff." It almost reads like a pep rally on paper. Each department gives a cleverly presented, upbeat overview of what's going on—where work stands in that department, what they are proud of, and news about individuals (marriages, births, outside accomplishments, and so on). Senior staff members and department heads make it a point to compliment or acknowledge individuals who may be cited in the newsletter.

Most of all, they build people's self-esteem by treating them with respect. They give them the tools they need to do their jobs, they give them a lot of freedom to be creative and then when they succeed, they shout it from the rooftops.

A Fun Work Environment

Having fun is a way of life at *Blue's Clues*—it's not something that is orchestrated or planned for. The senior staff sets an informal tone and has so much fun themselves that it is contagious. It just happens naturally. Well, it doesn't just happen—it is the by-product of a lot of things. It's a product of the disciplines they have in place and clear expectations, all of which free people to do good work. It's a function of the respect people have for one another and the safe, nurturing environment that has been created.

Blue's Clues is a very social organization. They celebrate just about everything and many of them are friends outside of work. Before an episode premieres, they all gather in one room and watch it together, pointing out each other's work, laughing hysterically as if they are seeing it through the eyes of preschoolers for the first time.

THE BOTTOM LINE

Leadership is much more than a skill. It is the essence of who the leaders are. It is the spirit and values the leaders bring to the workplace. When leaders have the right spirit, when they truly care about people and the people know it; when they have a strong vision and are able to communicate it; and when they put the management disciplines in place that free people to create great work, there is no limit to what a team can achieve.

CLUES FOR Leading People Effectively

Good leadership and management is as much about the person you are as it is the things that you do. Here are some things you can do to create a work environment that meets the needs of your team and the company while meeting the needs of employees:

- Make sure you have a clear vision, communicate it to your team, and keep them focused on it at all times.

- Empower your team by meeting their work needs so they can meet the needs of your customers.

- Clearly define the roles, responsibilities, and decision-making authority of individuals and departments.

- Make sure you have clearly defined, efficient work processes that facilitate high performance. Work with them to constantly monitor, evaluate, and refine the work processes.

- If you are managing your company, team, or department, make sure you and your peers are consistent in the way you manage. Also, work with one another the way you want your staff to work together.

- Keep giving people the big picture and keep them connected to the customer.

- Be honest with people and give them constructive feedback on a regular basis.

- Set high standards for people and provide them with the tools and support they need to reach them.

- Challenge people by giving them work that requires them to stretch and grow.

- Promote people from within when you can. Provide a development plan for everyone on your team.

- Maintain the proper balance between the needs of the people and the needs of the organization.

- Look for opportunities to praise people and teams.

- Help people and departments see how their job fits into the total picture.

- Celebrate the successes of your team.

- Admit your mistakes when you are wrong.

- Create an environment where people can have a good time while they are working.

- Respect people's personal lives and encourage them to maintain a healthy work–life balance.

CLUES FOR Leading Your Own Life and Career

In order to get where you want in your life, it's important that you take complete responsibility for your own happiness. As some have suggested, you have to be your own CEO. Here are some suggestions for getting to where you want to be:

- Make sure you have a clear vision of the life you want.

- Put together a plan for how you are going to get there.

- Identify the skills and competencies you will need to reach your goals.

- Develop a network and support system that can help you get to where you want to go.

- Be congruent in what you believe, what you say, and what you do so that people will trust you.

- Listen to your heart and trust your instincts.

- Give yourself permission to fail.

- Face your weaknesses and do something about them.

- Develop healthy relationships with other people. You need them to achieve your goals and to have a satisfying life.

- Use obstacles and setbacks as an opportunity to learn.

- Maintain the proper balance between your personal life and your work.

CHAPTER Summary

If a company is to realize its mission and maximize its potential, it must have a clear philosophy for managing people. The leaders of the organization must support one another if they expect people and departments to collaborate and support one another. The leaders must be consistent in the way they live the company's management philosophy in order for the people to trust them and want to follow them.

If the leaders of an organization care about the people, the people will care about their work and the customer. If the leaders put aside their own ego needs, focus on the mission, and work to build the self-esteem of the people they are leading, the people will return it with commitment and high performance.

Instead of focusing on the work, the leaders must focus on the needs of the people. If they do, the work will take care of itself. Leaders must tell people what their jobs are, give them the authority to do those jobs, communicate the standards and expectations, provide them with the information they need for wise decision making, train them to do their jobs, give them honest, direct feedback, and recognize them for their efforts. Leaders must be willing to look at themselves, admit their mistakes, and change. They must treat people with respect in order to get commitment and high performance from people.

Clue #7

When the *leadership* of your organization truly cares about people, when they consistently model the values and behaviors they want from others, when they treat people with respect and meet their work needs, the fulfillment of the mission and the accomplishment of your business objectives will be a natural by-product.

CHAPTER 8

Clue In to Your Culture

FOUNDATION FOR SUCCESS

The culture of any organization is a primary factor in its success or failure —it always finds its way to the bottom line. Leaders who recognize this fact make conscious decisions about what kind of culture will best support the company's business needs and objectives. They plan for it and manage it like they do every other aspect of the business.

Culture can be defined as the commonly held values, attitudes, and beliefs that drive the behavior of the people who work in the organization. It is the psychological, social, and emotional environment in which they work. The culture manifests itself in a multitude of ways: how people address one another in the hallways, how they resolve conflict, how they dress, and how they make decisions. It pervades virtually everything about an organization, which is why it is difficult to manage and even more difficult to change.

CULTURES WITHIN A CULTURE

The *Blue's Clues* culture was actually born out of the Nick Jr. and Nickelodeon cultures. While there are differences between the three cultures, certain defining characteristics run through all three. Those characteristics are the foundation for Nickelodeon's long-term success as the number-one entertainment company for kids and the most watched cable network in the country. Nick Jr. is the gold standard for preschool children's television programming and *Blue's Clues* is a true phenomenon on its way to becoming a classic, largely because of the following cultural characteristics:

Kid focused. Everything they do is about looking at the world from a kid's point of view. As communicated in Nickelodeon's mission statement, it is about connecting with kids and helping kids connect to their world through entertainment. Decisions are always based on what's good for kids and what kids want.

Process as important as the product. They believe that how they get to the end product is as important as the end product itself. They are very clear about how people should treat one another and work together. They try to model what they put on the air. If they want kids to respect themselves they know they have to respect one another.

Risk taking. Creativity is all about breaking rules and going outside the boundaries. They try a lot of stuff that doesn't work. Ideas are highly valued no matter who or where they come from. People are encouraged to take risks and stretch themselves. There are no penalties for trying something new and failing.

Research based. Few entertainment companies do as much research as Nickelodeon, Nick Jr., and *Blue's Clues*. They are a true fact-based company. They never assume that they know what kids are thinking or feeling.

Team oriented. Just about everything happens in teams. The work process is highly collaborative; it has to be in order to produce brilliant creative work that also accomplishes the company's business objectives. Teamwork is about valuing everybody's opinion, not letting hierarchies get in the way, and letting information flow freely.

Creatively driven. It's a place where creativity comes before business. In other words, they don't let the bottom line dictate to the creative. Creativity comes first, enabling them to accomplish their business objectives. It's a place where creative people, regardless of title or rank, are able to flourish.

Diverse and inclusive. They believe the world is a rich and complicated place. They embrace all aspects of diversity, creating a wide variety of experiences for kids and showing kids of all races, ages, abilities, religions, and personalities on the network. And to create programming that reflects diversity, they employ a diverse workforce.

Attention to work place environment. A lot of time and resources are spent creating work environments that feed peoples' creative juices. There are giant chalkboards from ceiling to floor for creating and doodling. The furniture and walls are in bright, primary colors. The work space design is open and spacious, and facilitates teamwork.

Fun. People try to stay in touch with the kid inside themselves. One way they do that is by creating a fun work environment. If the people creating the product aren't having fun, they will have difficulty creating a fun experience for their audiences.

The following message appeared on the Nick Jr.
Web site message board for parents:

Steve Helped My Son!

   I just wanted to let Steve know how much he
has helped my son! My little boy is two and a
half and was having a hard time talking.
Basically, he didn't talk at all! Finally, he
started getting into *Blue's Clues* and within a
couple of weeks he was saying "Steve," "Blue,"
"Mailbox," and "Shovel." I was so impressed
with the way that Steve really seemed to teach
my child. Jacob has even learned signs from
him! Thank you, Steve!

Learning. Learning and development are highly valued. People are given all kinds of opportunities to stretch and acquire new skills—from attending symposiums and training classes, to listening to outside speakers, to having a mentor, to getting a new position outside of their area of expertise.

THE TRUE TEST OF A CULTURE

Every organization, regardless of how enlightened, claims to have lofty values. Too often these are empty words on a page. The *Blue's Clues* story has been told here in great detail, but the real story of a company's culture can best be told by its employees. I gathered a large group of *Blue's Clues* employees in a conference room, turned on the tape recorder, and asked each to tell his or her story. These stories might help you, the reader, understand and feel what it is like to work there. The following stories are presented as they were told.

PERSONAL STORIES

One of the things I like about working at Blue's Clues *is that you don't get pigeonholed. You get to try new things and stretch yourself. If you learn about the work of another department and have the skill to participate in their work, you can take on special assignments on your own time. You have to prove that you can do the work, but the opportunities are there.*

For a long time, I wanted to write an episode—but, of course, that wasn't my "job." Finally, one day I got up the nerve to tell my boss that I had an idea for an episode and told her about it. As a researcher I had demonstrated some writing skill, so she said, "Why don't you write it up?" Before I knew it I was teamed up with one of the scriptwriters who walked me through the process and together we wrote an episode. It was such a high!

Since that time I have written another episode on my own and I have even written some books. The opportunities to grow here are endless!

Alison Sherman
Research

When I first joined Blue's Clues *as an animator I was working on a temporary student visa. I had applied for a longer-term visa, but my first visa ran out so I had to go back to my homeland, Israel, until it was approved. When I left I*

didn't know how long it would take and neither did Blue's Clues. *They didn't want me to be without employment while I was gone so they set me up with a computer, let me work from home, and paid me as though I was in the office. Nickelodeon went to great lengths to get my visa approved, which came through about four months later. I feel a real debt of gratitude for that.*

I have also been supported in other ways. A few years after I had been working at Blue's Clues *I had a feature film script accepted by the Sundance Film Makers Lab. It was a huge honor. It was one of eight scripts selected from over 3,000. It meant that I would have the opportunity to go to the Sundance Institute for a total of six weeks to shoot the scenes working under the guidance of some of the top filmmakers in the country. Not only did* Blue's Clues *give me the time off, but they also cheered me on.*

Tatia Rosenthal
Animation

*B*efore I changed career paths and became an animator, I worked in corporate sales so I have a lot with which to compare my experience at* Blue's Clues. *I have attended a lot of success seminars, many of which talk about one of the principles in Napoleon Hill's book,* Think and Grow Rich—*the principle of the mastermind group.*

One of the reasons for our phenomenal success is the way the leaders of Blue's Clues *apply the mastermind concept. They apply it better than any company I have ever seen. Not only are they incredibly focused but they have created a very nurturing environment where all of the departments within the company work in harmony with each other. Peoples' egos rarely get in the way of the work; everyone just wants to create great work for our audience, the kids.*

Blue's Clues *is a very high-energy place but, in contrast to many companies where the anxiety level is unnecessarily high,* Blue's Clues *is a very peaceful place to work. I especially appreciate that because it frees my mind to focus on my work and be creative.*

Andrew Levin
Animation

*O*ne of the things that is interesting about Blue's Clues *is that six of the eight members of our senior staff are women. Somehow they are able to strike an amazing balance between what we think of as masculine qualities— achievement, goal orientation, assertiveness—and feminine qualities— imagination, nurturing, and relationship building.*

My own manager is my role model for just that reason. I have seen her in some very tough situations with people outside of the production; and she is a perfect example of grace under fire. She can take a lot of heat and never lose her cool. I have also seen her make some very tough calls with employees, and tackle issues with them that most managers would back away from.

At the same time my manager is very nurturing. Whenever she gives me my review, her first questions are always, "How are you doing and where do you want to go from here?" I always feel that my growth and career satisfaction are just as important to her as getting the work done. Not only is she a great leader, but so are the other members of the senior management. They all do an exemplary job of staying balanced, accomplishing the goal and nurturing the people at the same time.

Marcy Pritchard
Production

Sometimes we have such a good time at work it hardly feels like work. We do a lot of crazy things and have a lot of laughs while we are getting our work done. One of the funniest times I remember was a party we had planned for one of the designers who was leaving the show. We thought of how cool it would be if we had someone dressed as Blue come to the party.

At the time we didn't have a character costume so we got the idea of calling a local costume shop. If they had one, of course, it would not have been authorized by Blue's Clues, but we called anyway. We didn't tell the costume shop where we were from—we just said we were a children's television show.

When the actor arrived in costume at the security desk downstairs and found out who the client was, he ran out of the building and called his office from a pay phone across the street. "Why didn't you tell me I was going to Blue's Clues?" he screamed. The net of it all was that we had one of the creators draw up a release form saying that he could play Blue and wear the costume for that one day, after which time he would never do it again. So he came to the party but he was a lousy Blue. We tried to teach him to bark like Blue but he just couldn't get it. On top of it all, we couldn't get him to leave.

Michael Lapinski
Digital Design

One of the interesting things about Blue's Clues is that there is a lot of movement from department to department. If you want another job in the company badly enough, you usually get it. If you master the job you are in and take the initiative to learn as much as you can about the job you want, management will go to great lengths to see that you get there, even if it means some work and inconvenience for them.

I had been a storyboard artist for quite some time and had mastered the job. I was ready for a new challenge and really wanted to be an animator—it was my dream. Management could have easily ignored my request, but because I had performed well, they went to the trouble of interviewing and hiring someone for the job I was doing. They put together a plan for my transition and trained me for the new position. I think that is one of the reasons the turnover is so low here and why people are so loyal. Everybody just keeps growing—we don't get bored and stale in our jobs because we are constantly given new challenges.

David Levy
Animation

I absolutely love coming to work every day. One reason I like it is because it feels like family—a healthy family. We can disagree and have our opinions but you don't have all the undercurrents that you find in a lot of companies. People really work at getting along and supporting one another.

Speaking of family, I happen to have a six-year-old little brother, James, who is not only a big fan of the show but he loves to come to the office to visit me. Sometimes my mother drops him off on a Friday so he can spend the weekend with me. On one particular occasion we were celebrating a Blue's Clues milestone.

I brought James to work with me on that particular day (there aren't many places you can bring a sibling to work) and it wasn't long before he disappeared. At one point I turned around and there he was, flying down the hallways in a swivel chair with two pieces of cake in his lap, laughing hysterically. A little later I saw him and I hardly recognized him—someone had spiked his hair. My little brother had been "adopted" by my coworkers and was having the time of his life. He keeps asking me when he can come back to my office. He says, "I like it there because people love me a lot."

Astrid Riemer
Art and Design

*O*ne of the reasons I think we are successful in creating Blue's Clues is be-cause we all try very hard to stay connected to the three- or four-year-old within ourselves. In fact, when people are hired to work here it is always with the eye of determining whether someone has a real "kid sensibility." It's a strange line that we walk—we have to stay childlike when we do our work but we also have to be very responsible. Unless you enjoy managing yourself you don't make it here.

We all have pictures of ourselves when we were little tacked to a big wall in the office. Most people's offices have somewhere displayed their favorite toys and icons when they were kids. And you wouldn't believe the endless conversations we have about how we felt, how we saw the world, what made us afraid, what made us happy when we were little—all as a way of trying to remember what it felt like at that age so we can create a show that is both fun and educational for kids.

Soo Kim
Digital Design

I have always been impressed by how much people support one another around here but I guess I never really realized just how much they cared until I had a bad automobile accident, which kept me out of work for three months.

While I was in the hospital they kept my spirits up with lots of visits. Hardly a day went by when someone from the office didn't come to see me. After I left the hospital I went to stay with my parents in Connecticut, where streams of people continued to visit, which was surprising when you consider how far it is from New York City. Even Steve made the trip. One day the entire writing department came and put on a mock Blue's Clues episode, in which they had done parodies of past episodes I had written.

The first day I returned to the office, tears came to my eyes when I saw what they had done. My office was decorated with balloons and streamers and all *kinds of "welcome back" messages. And they had completely rearranged my office so it would be easy for me to work. Since I was on crutches I couldn't get up to get my morning and afternoon tea so they had even bought me a little hot pot, which was sitting on my desk. The whole experience was one I will never forget.*

Jessica Lissy
Writing

*O*ne of the bonuses for me in working at Blue's Clues *is that it makes my parents so proud. My mother is an artist and my father works in the television industry, so they have a real appreciation for what I do as an artist on the show.*

A few years ago I went to my parents' house to watch one of Blue's Clues *prime-time specials with them. The show was about the birth of a new character, Paprika, who was the daughter of Mr. Salt and Mrs. Pepper. It was the first time I had played a major role in creating a new character. The episode was sweet and sensitive, designed to help preschoolers get excited and adjust to having a new baby in the house.*

While we were watching the show I glanced over at my parents and they both had tears in their eyes. They were so proud of me and so happy that I had found work that I love so much. And then I started crying and the whole family was crying.

When I go into a toy store with my mother to buy gifts for my niece, I sometimes have to hide because she tells everyone in the store that her son works for Blue's Clues. *On one particular occasion as I left the store, two young sales clerks came up and asked for my autograph. It was the first time I have ever felt like a celebrity.*

Ian Chernichaw
Art and Design

If anyone ever listened in on any of our meetings, they might think we were a bit strange. We can be very serious about things like whether or not one of the characters should have a nose or if it should have hair and if so, what color. Sometimes we crack up when we hear ourselves talk, because it's as though we are right there, living in the fantasy world we are creating.

We get very excited about the worlds we create. The skidoos are particularly fun. In every episode Joe and Blue skidoo to an exciting new place and, as we create the adventures, it's as though we get to go on them, too. I remember once we created a skidoo to a marina where we taught kids about boats. Our excitement grew with every detail as we worked together to enhance the scene.

We also get very attached to the characters we create. There was the episode we did about feelings and how to handle them. During the skidoo, the audience met a character named Felix who was sad and another character named Trevor who was worried. Our favorite though was a little girl named Mary Ann who was angry. For some reason we got attached to Mary Ann. Maybe because we got to express that side of ourselves through her. Through her we also learned what to do when we get angry. It's amazing what we learn—what we are reminded of as we create the show.

Amanda Lattrell
Art and Design

Most of the time we really do get into the spirit of what we do. A few years ago, we did a prime-time special, Blue's Big Pajama Party. *As part of the promotion, families were encouraged to go to their television sets in their pajamas the evening of the show, and everyone at* Blue's Clues *was encouraged to go to work in their pajamas the day it aired.*

I was really into that episode and the promotion because I was the animator who animated the characters wearing their pajamas on the show. I wore a leopard-print nightgown and some fuzzy slippers. It was fun to make people smile and to be introduced to visitors in the office with the disclaimer, "He doesn't usually dress this way."

Around midday a group of us walked five or six blocks in our pajamas to the Viacom Building, where Nickelodeon is headquartered. We had a milk-and-cookies party while we watched the finished show. Nickelodeon President Herb Scannell also came to the viewing in his pajamas.

As I walked down Broadway to the building, I expected a few chuckles or stares, but nothing much is strange to New Yorkers. Instead I was interviewed on an Italian television broadcast, which just happened to be on the street. They made sure to get a good shot of my legs.

Dale Clowdis
Animation

I think one reason we are able to create such good work is because of the relationships we have with one another. It's almost like college in some ways. Some of us even room together. One of my best friends works in another department—we "jam" about work constantly when we are not at work, which I think really helps to enhance the end product. We know each other so well that when we pass our work onto each other we instinctively know what the other will do with it next. We respect each other's work so much that we never want to pass on work to the other that isn't our absolute best.

Most of the people who work here are such good friends that it's hard to tell where work ends and the personal begins. We have our own offices, but people are constantly flowing in and out. Everywhere you look, people are working in groups. After work, it's not unusual to see people hanging out, playing cards or chess. We have a number of people who are musicians so sometimes you'll see people jamming on their guitars. When Monsters Inc. came out, about 15 animators went to see it together. One of the benefits of working here is that you almost have a built-in social life.

Scott Dodson
Art and Design

*O*ne time, someone was interviewing for a job here and commented, "This place is like a country unto its own. You have your own language and vocabulary. It's different from anything I've ever seen or heard." When I think about it, the person is right. We do have our own unique way of communicating. We use words like "biggerize," which means to make larger. Or "perspecterize," which means to show an object from a different angle. Or "yummify," which means to take something, say an apple, which looks normal and ordinary, and give it a heightened reality so that it is, for example, redder and shinier, so that the viewer wants to grab it right out of the screen.*

We are also quite visceral in the way we communicate. We use a lot of hand gestures and sounds—gestures and sounds that are understood by almost everyone—when we want to communicate something that we can't quite put into words. And then we have our somewhat offbeat sayings and quotes, original quotes by people who work in the office.

It's true that we have our own way of communicating, but at the same time there is a lot of room for individuality. At a lot of companies you have to carefully edit every thought before you speak and there is a prescribed way of speaking but not here. It's one of the joys of working at Blue's Clues.

Alex Fogarty
Digital Design

The loss of a parent is a difficult experience for anyone. When my mother was diagnosed with cancer after I had been working at Blue's Clues for a year, I was devastated. There were times when I didn't know how I would get through it. The outpouring of love and compassion from my coworkers during that time was what got me through on many days. It was like nothing I had ever experienced before. Even my family and friends were flabbergasted.

During my mother's nine-month illness, I wanted to be with her as much as I could. Whenever there was a doctor's appointment, a test—and there were many—I never even had to ask for the time off. It was just understood that that's what I should do. My boss could not have been more understanding. When my mother passed away, my coworkers reached out to me in so many ways. The art department made this beautiful, intricately designed card, which had a picture of Blue in the Thinking Chair. The card said "We are thinking of you." Inside, my coworkers had written the most thoughtful messages.

My parents' home is over an hour away from the office, but that didn't stop a large group of people from coming to the funeral. One evening when we were sitting shiva, another large group of people came, some who I hardly knew, and listened as my father told stories about my mother. People from the office donated thousands of dollars in my mother's name to a cancer fund—we are a relatively small office of mostly young people in their 20s and early 30s. After my mother died and I felt I needed to take a few weeks off, again, there was only encouragement to do so. The day I returned to the office one of the creators had made me a big pan of lasagna for my dinner that night.

But it doesn't stop there. Months later, a group of people in the office walked in a candlelight walk for cancer in New York City in my mother's name, and when the anniversary of her death came around, they were there too: more cards letting me know they were thinking of me. I know it's a story that is hard to believe, but it's true. The loss of my mother was hard and still is, but my *heart is so warm and full of love because of what the people I work with have done for me.*

Karen Leavitt
Research

*I*t's a good feeling going to work every day, knowing that you are doing work that is significant. Once we did an episode on sounds, in which we introduced preschoolers to all kinds of sounds and where they come from. Some of the sounds were those associated with thunderstorms. One day after the episode aired, one of my coworkers who has a little boy thanked me for writing that episode. He said, "My son used to be terrified of thunder and lightning. A few days after he saw the episode there was a storm. He started to get frightened and then he remembered the show and was perfectly calm."

Once I was at a gathering of friends and family where I met a precocious four-year-old little girl who was a huge fan of the show. As we chatted about different episodes and characters, she recounted story lines I had written and recalled details even I had forgotten. When our conversation turned to one of the characters, Periwinkle, who I had played a major role in developing, she got very excited. She obviously adored Periwinkle and spoke about him as if she knew him, as if he was a friend of hers.

When we have encounters like these or when we go to the live theatrical show, we realize this thing we create called Blue's Clues has a life of its own. It's like a living being. We realize that the fantasy world we work to create every day is a powerful reality for preschoolers everywhere. There aren't many places you can get those kinds of rewards from your work.

Adam Peltzman
Writing

A lot of people around our office are artists of some sort. In addition to their work on the show, most of them are always working on their own outside projects—producing short films, painting, singing in bands, or soloing in clubs— we have a very talented group here. The interesting thing is that management encourages us to do outside projects. A lot of companies might frown on outside projects, but the way they look at it, the more creative we are in other parts of our life, the more creativity we will be able to bring to our work at Blue's Clues.

We even have a Nick digital animation festival. Animators from Blue's Clues and other Nickelodeon shows are invited to submit their outside projects as a way of showcasing their work to their peers. After a special viewing during work hours, it is shown on a closed-circuit television in the lobby over a period of days.

When someone's work wins an award or when someone has the opportunity to participate in a competition, not only is management supportive, but coworkers cheer them on as well. If someone is singing in a club, it's not unusual for the audience to consist of a whole group of people from the office. When one of our employees was performing at a club in Brooklyn, the animation department even developed some animation, which ran in the background as she sang. The creative process can be very frustrating, but when you have a group of people always encouraging you, it helps you to stick with it and believe in your work even more.

David Bouffard
Editing

*I*t's funny how you can tell a lot about a company when you first walk in the door. Before anyone says a word, you get a feeling—vibes if you will—of what the place is all about. From the moment I walked in the door at Blue's Clues for my interview, I knew it was my dream job.

The first thing I noticed when I walked in the door was that the environment was so friendly and welcoming. In the lobby there was a large screen TV playing Nickelodeon shows, there were tables in the shape of flowers, the wallpaper was of clouds, and the reception desk looked like an aquarium. The walls inside the office were colored in vivid hues of blue, orange, and yellow. And there were toys everywhere—action figures of all kinds, stuffed animals, even a piñata—everything you could think of. The people and environment looked so fun and creative.

When the interview started, I couldn't believe how friendly everyone was. Before they even offered me the job I was escorted around the office and introduced to people, including the creators. Everyone made me feel so welcome. It's been about a year and a half now, and I still pinch myself. I feel so fortunate to be able to work at such a special place.

Khalida Katy Lockheed
Digital Design

I'm not that old but I'm older than most people at Blue's Clues, *so I have a lot of prior work experience. Believe me, I know what we have here. One of the things that struck me when I first came to work here was how open everyone was and how there were no layers. You could talk to anyone about anything, regardless of their title, something I had never experienced in all the jobs I had before. I remember one day not long after I had been working here, one of the creators came into my office, asked me how I was doing and if I had everything I needed to do my job. She sat down and chatted with me for a while and then went on her way. I thought I would fall off my chair, I was so pleasantly surprised.*

Perhaps the thing I appreciate most is that you don't have to wear a mask here or assume a "work persona." If you are having a bad day, you can say you are having a bad day. You don't have to play the game, which I found exhausting at other places I worked, places where you always had to walk the fine line, dress the way they expected you to dress, speak the way they wanted you to speak. People here are of a similar spirit and work ethic but beyond that it is a very diverse place. There is tremendous room for self-expression in all its forms.

One more benefit—we all get a call from Blue on our birthday!

John Terhorst
Archives

*W*hen I came to work at Blue's Clues *upon graduating from college, I was so excited to find a job that I could look forward to going to each morning. I had studied psychology and art and had a big interest in child development, so the job seemed like a perfect match.*

But there was something else I noticed from the moment I walked in the door—it was the people. It was amazing to be around such a committed, passionate group of people. No one seemed to be just doing a "job." Everyone seemed to be fully invested in what they were doing and enjoying it, at every level.

One reason I think we have been so successful is because our leaders and everyone else are constantly asking the question, "How can we make it better?" It's just the way we think. We have set a standard for excellence here that is quite rare. One of the things I have gained from working here is an appreciation for what it takes to be a success—for one, it takes a tremendous amount of attention to detail.

The other thing I have learned is the importance of having a vision. Because our leaders are so clear about what the show should be and where it is going, it makes our jobs so much easier. It's a lesson in clarity—the clearer you are about what you want, the greater the likelihood you are going to get it.

Sarah Landy
Production

CLUES FOR Building a Culture That Is Right for Your Company

The culture that is right for one company may not be right for another. The important thing is to recognize its importance and never assume that because you see the world or the company in a certain way that the people who work for you see it the same way. Although the signs of an organization's culture are everywhere, it can be quite elusive because it isn't concrete. Here are some recommendations to ensure that you have the kind of culture you need to support the mission and goals of your business:

- Determine what you would like your culture to be. In a perfect world, what would it look like?

- Identify the key behaviors you want people to demonstrate.

- Identify the values, attitudes, and beliefs that would predispose people to demonstrating the behaviors you desire.

- Do an assessment of where your culture is today relative to where you want it to be.

- Put together a comprehensive plan for moving your company closer to the culture you desire.

- As you develop the plan, consider all of the ways you communicate to employees and the messages that are being sent. Look to see where they are receiving mixed messages.

- Develop an orientation program that communicates your culture to new employees.

- Hold managers accountable for living true to the company's values.

- Reward people for living the company's values.

- Continuously monitor the health of your culture.

As you assess your culture and develop plans for changing it, you will want to involve the people of the organization in the process. If they are involved in defining the culture they would like to have, they will be more invested in making it happen.

CLUES FOR Determining If Your Company's Culture Is Right for You

Sometimes people are unhappy in their jobs because they don't fit with the culture of the company where they are working. The job may be right but not the culture. Here arc some questions to help you determine if the culture where you work is a fit for you:

- Do you feel you are able to be yourself at work or do you feel that you have to twist yourself like a pretzel in order to fit in?

- What does the executive management of your company valuc? Do their values fit with your values?

- Are you proud of the company for which you work?

- Do you feel in sync or out of sync with your coworkers?

- Do you look forward to going to work in the morning? If not, why not?

- Do you feel you have to watch what you say at work or do you feel you can speak freely?

- What are the things about your company that you like and dislike?

- If you could change the culture of your company in any way, how would you change it?

CHAPTER Summary

The culture of any organization is the summation of the common attitudes, values, and beliefs held by the people of the organization, which predispose them to behave in certain ways. Leaders must pay attention to the culture of their organization and be clear about what kind of culture they need in order for the company to meet its business objectives. The culture of an organization should be managed just like every other aspect of the business. The leaders of the organization must model the attitudes, values, and behaviors they want the rest of the organization to exhibit.

Everything a company does communicates a message that either reinforces or detracts from the desired culture. In order to move the culture of an organization to a better place, a thorough analysis should be done of the present culture. If there is a real disparity between the present culture and what they wish the culture to be, an ongoing plan should be established for moving the company closer to that culture. The health of the culture should be monitored on a consistent basis.

Clue #8

The *culture* of your organization is the environment in which people live. If it is a healthy environment, if it is one that the leaders plan for and carefully manage, the people will flourish and so will the business.

CHAPTER 9

The Thinking Chair

I hope you have enjoyed the *Blue's Clues* story. I have covered a lot of information but I hope you received at least one message: When a small group of people have a powerful vision, when they are able to put their egos aside for their vision, when they have a genuine love and respect for one another and for what they do, there is no limit to what they can achieve. As the anthropologist Margaret Mead said, "Never doubt that a small group of thoughtful, committed people can change the world. Indeed, it is the only thing that ever has."

Toward the end of every *Blue's Clues* episode, the live-action host goes to his big red Thinking Chair and asks the preschoolers watching at home to "Think! Think! Think!" It's the cue for the kids to think about the three clues they have discovered throughout the show so they can solve the puzzle. When they shout out the answer and the live-action host tells them how smart they are, it's a true moment of celebration. At a young age, they are being taught to reflect and analyze, something that is fairly uncommon in our fast-paced, activity-driven culture, particularly in the corporate world.

I hope you will take some time to reflect on *Blue's Clues for Success,* whether in your business or on a personal level. In terms of business, I hope you will think hard about the following:

Clue #1. A clear and powerful MISSION provides the focus for mobilizing the energy of your people. If it is one they can believe in, you can win their hearts as well as their minds, which is essential to your business success.

Clue #2. When you know your CUSTOMER, love your customer, and keep him or her the FOCUS of everything you do, you won't have to worry about the competition. You will be in a class of your own.

Clue #3. RESEARCH is the tool that keeps you connected to your customer and aligned with your mission. When you use research for the basis of your decision making, you will be able to meet the needs of your customer with amazing precision.

Clue #4. When you are the master of your TECHNOLOGY and you use it creatively to accomplish your business objectives, it can empower you to do things for your customer that no one else has done.

Clue # 5. Effective WORK PROCESSES are the key to quality, high performance, and efficiency. When the people of the organization help to create processes that work, they are empowered to meet the objectives of the organization.

Clue #6. When you are crystal clear about who and what you want to be in the mind of your customer, and you manage every detail of your business so that customers see you as being in a class of your own, you will have BRANDED your product.

Clue #7. When the LEADERSHIP of your organization truly cares about people, when they consistently model the values and behaviors they want from others, when they treat people with respect and meet their work needs, the fulfillment of the mission and the accomplishment of your business objectives will be a natural by-product.

Clue #8. The CULTURE of your organization is the environment in which people live. If it is a healthy environment—if it is one that the leaders plan for and manage carefully—the people will flourish and so will the business.

Throughout this book, I hope you have gotten some clues for your personal life as well. I hope the stories by the people responsible for the success of *Blue's Clues* have inspired you in some way. I hope you will reflect on and remember the following:

- If you have a strong vision and a mission for your life, there is no limit to what you can achieve.

- If you don't have a mission for your life, if you don't have work that you love, don't settle until you find it. If you do, you will die with all your greatness within you.

- Have the courage to be your own unique self and don't be afraid to break the rules.

- Listen to your heart—it knows better than your head what is best for you.

- Be willing to pay the price for a rich, satisfying life; but the harder the climb, the sweeter the success.

- Refuse to be defined by your past or the struggles you have encountered along the way.

The staff that brings laughter to millions of preschoolers. (Show host Donovan Patton, "Joe," seated on floor at far right.)

- Give yourself permission to fail; allow yourself to be human. Failure is inherent in almost every great achievement.

- Build strong, healthy bonds with other people. You need them to reach your full potential and it makes the journey a whole lot more fulfilling.

And last, remember the *Blue's Clues* line: "When you use your mind, take a step at a time, you can do anything that you want to do."

Author Diane Tracy is an internationally recognized speaker, author, and executive coach for Fortune 500 companies and beyond. Her clients include organizations such as MTV, AT&T, Bristol-Myers Squibb, HBO, and the Social Security Administration. Her books, which have been translated into many foreign languages, include *Truth, Trust, and the Bottom Line, Take This Job and Love It, The 10 Steps to Empowerment,* and *The First Book of Common Sense Management.* For information on services provided by her company, Tracy Communications, contact <www.DianeTracy.info>.

Director of Research and Development Alice Wilder, cocreator Traci Paige Johnson, author Diane Tracy, Animation Director Dave Palmer, cocreator Angela Santomero, and Executive Producer Jennifer Twomey (kneeling) with son Ethan, future *Blue's Clues* fan.

CLUE IN YOUR WHOLE ORGANIZATION!

For quantities of
Blue's Clues for Success,
please contact Mindi Rowland
in Special Sales,
800-621-9621, ext. 4410,
rowland@dearborn.com.

Your company also can order
this book with a
customized cover featuring
your name, logo, and message.

Dearborn™
Trade Publishing
A **Kaplan Professional** Company